COLLINS
CHEERFUL
COOKING

SIMPLE
FAMILY
MEALS

© Wm. Collins Sons & Co. Ltd. 1973
First published 1973
ISBN 0 00 435270 X

Devised, edited and designed by Youé & Spooner Ltd.

Printed in Great Britain by Collins Clear-Type Press

COLLINS
CHEERFUL
COOKING

SIMPLE
FAMILY
MEALS

SUSAN GRAHAM

COLLINS
LONDON & GLASGOW

Useful weights and measures

WEIGHT EQUIVALENTS

Avoirdupois		Metric
1 ounce	=	28·35 grammes
1 pound	=	453·6 grammes
2·3 pounds	=	1 kilogram

LIQUID MEASUREMENTS

$\frac{1}{4}$ pint	=	1$\frac{1}{2}$ decilitres
$\frac{1}{2}$ pint	=	$\frac{1}{4}$ litre
scant 1 pint	=	$\frac{1}{2}$ litre
1$\frac{3}{4}$ pints	=	1 litre
1 gallon	=	4·5 litres

HANDY LIQUID MEASURES

1 pint	=	20 fluid ounces	=	32 tablespoons
$\frac{1}{2}$ pint	=	10 fluid ounces	=	16 tablespoons
$\frac{1}{4}$ pint	=	5 fluid ounces	=	8 tablespoons
$\frac{1}{8}$ pint	=	2$\frac{1}{2}$ fluid ounces	=	4 tablespoons
$\frac{1}{16}$ pint	=	1$\frac{1}{4}$ fluid ounces	=	2 tablespoons

HANDY SOLID MEASURES

				Approximate
Almonds, ground	1 oz.	=	3$\frac{3}{4}$	level tablespoons
Arrowroot	1 oz.	=	4	level tablespoons
Breadcrumbs fresh	1 oz.	=	7	level tablespoons
dried	1 oz.	=	3$\frac{1}{4}$	level tablespoons
Butter and Lard	1 oz.	=	2	level tablespoons
Cheese, grated	1 oz.	=	3$\frac{1}{2}$	level tablespoons
Chocolate, grated	1 oz.	=	3	level tablespoons
Cocoa	1 oz.	=	2$\frac{3}{4}$	level tablespoons
Desiccated Coconut	1 oz.	=	4$\frac{1}{2}$	tablespoons
Coffee—Instant	1 oz.	=	4	level tablespoons
Ground	1 oz.	=	4	tablespoons
Cornflour	1 oz.	=	2$\frac{1}{2}$	tablespoons
Custard powder	1 oz.	=	2$\frac{1}{2}$	tablespoons
Curry Powder and Spices	1 oz.	=	5	tablespoons
Flour	1 oz.	=	2	level tablespoons
Gelatine, powdered	1 oz.	=	2$\frac{1}{2}$	tablespoons
Rice, uncooked	1 oz.	=	1$\frac{1}{2}$	tablespoons
Sugar, caster and granulated	1 oz.	=	2	tablespoons
Icing sugar	1 oz.	=	2$\frac{1}{2}$	tablespoons
Syrup	1 oz.	=	1	tablespoon
Yeast, granulated	1 oz.	=	1	level tablespoon

AMERICAN MEASURES

16 fluid ounces	=	1 American pint
8 fluid ounces	=	1 American standard cup
0·50 fluid ounces	=	1 American tablespoon (slightly smaller than British Standards Institute tablespoon)
0·16 fluid ounces	=	1 American teaspoon

AUSTRALIAN MEASURES
(Cup, Spoon and Liquid Measures)

These are the measures in everyday use in the Australian family kitchen. The spoon measures listed below are from the ordinary household cutlery set.

CUP MEASURES

(Using the 8-liquid-ounce cup measure)

1 cup flour	4 oz.
1 cup sugar *(crystal or caster)*	8 oz.
1 cup icing sugar *(free from lumps)*	5 oz.
1 cup shortening *(butter, margarine, etc.)*	8 oz.
1 cup honey, golden syrup, treacle	10 oz.
1 cup brown sugar *(lightly packed)*	4 oz.
1 cup brown sugar *(tightly packed)*	5 oz.
1 cup soft breadcrumbs	2 oz.
1 cup dry breadcrumbs *(made from fresh breadcrumbs)*	3 oz.
1 cup packet dry breadcrumbs	4 oz.
1 cup rice *(uncooked)*	6 oz.
1 cup rice *(cooked)*	5 oz.
1 cup mixed fruit or individual fruit such as sultanas, etc.	4 oz.
1 cup grated cheese	4 oz.
1 cup nuts *(chopped)*	4 oz.
1 cup coconut	2$\frac{1}{2}$ oz.

SPOON MEASURES

	Level Tablespoon
1 oz. flour	2
1 oz. sugar *(crystal or caster)*	1$\frac{1}{2}$
1 oz. icing sugar *(free from lumps)*	2
1 oz. shortening	1
1 oz. honey	1
1 oz. gelatine	2
1 oz. cocoa	3
1 oz. cornflour	2$\frac{1}{2}$
1 oz. custard powder	2$\frac{1}{2}$

LIQUID MEASURES

(Using 8-liquid-ounce cup)

1 cup liquid	8 oz
2$\frac{1}{2}$ cups liquid	20 oz. (1 pint)
2 tablespoons liquid	1 oz.
1 gill liquid	5 oz. ($\frac{1}{4}$ pint)

Metric equivalents and oven temperatures are not listed here as they are included in all the recipes throughout the book.

When using the metric measures, in some cases it may be necessary to cut down the amount of liquid used. This is in order to achieve a balanced recipe and the correct consistency, as 1oz equals, in fact, 28·35gm.

Introduction

As a housewife, it's time I'm most short of! The days fly by and no matter how busy I am, nothing ever seems to damp the family's appetite. It's so easy to run out of ideas of what to give the family to eat, so I've written this book to help. It's full of quick-to-prepare recipes, many incorporating modern, convenience foods. Some may take a little while to cook, but all the recipes are simple and satisfying family fare and every recipe is based on readily available ingredients.

I hope I practise what I preach! I am a trained home economist married to a busy lawyer who often has irregular hours. I have a hungry schoolboy son and a small daughter who is very selective in her likes and dislikes! Running a fair-sized house, keeping a big garden neat and tidy, growing most of my own vegetables and fruit, teaching sewing once a week and writing in my spare time keeps me fairly busy, so I hope I know something about cooking simple meals!

I was Cookery Editor of a leading weekly magazine, then of two monthly magazines and finally wrote for a Sunday newspaper.

Since I was trained so many aids for the busy housewife have arrived on the scene. Supermarket shelves bulge with ready-cooked foods in cans and packets, and using these can help you cut down the time it takes you to prepare a meal. Keep a few at home to help you out in an emergency. Most of us now have a refrigerator in which we can keep a small stock of basic necessities to fall back on. Some of us are lucky enough to have freezers. We are living in an age where gadgets galore abound in an effort to make life easier.

My advice for painless meal preparation is to try to think at least one day ahead, to make the most of your kitchen gadgets and equipment and to keep a well stocked emergency shelf.

Good cooking!

Susan Graham

Eggs and cheese

Cheese and eggs don't take kindly to long cooking so they provide the basis of many good, nourishing and quick meals.

ASPARAGUS OMELETTE
Serves 2

1 can asparagus, drained
4 eggs
salt and pepper
1 tablespoon water
1 teaspoon chopped parsley
1½oz (37gm) butter

1. Turn the asparagus into a pan and heat through gently. Keep hot.
2. Break the eggs into a bowl, add seasoning, water and parsley. Beat very lightly with a fork.
3. Heat half the butter in an 8-inch (20cm) omelette pan. Pour in half the egg mixture and stir several times.
4. Leave the omelette to set, and brown a little.
5. Spoon half the asparagus on the omelette and fold in three.
6. Serve at once on a hot dish.
7. Repeat to make a second omelette.

SAVOURY OMELETTE WITH GARLIC TOAST
Serves 2

2 small onions
1 green pepper
1 red pepper
4 tomatoes
3oz (75gm) unsalted butter
1 garlic clove, crushed
6 eggs
3 tablespoons milk
salt and pepper
small pieces of toast spread with butter flavoured with crushed garlic

1. Skin and slice the onions.
2. Shred the peppers and discard the seeds.
3. Skin the tomatoes by dipping them in boiling water; remove seeds and chop flesh roughly.
4. Heat the butter in a frying pan and stir in the onion, peppers and garlic.
5. Cook slowly for 5 minutes without browning.
6. Lightly beat the eggs in a bowl with milk and seasoning.
7. Add tomatoes to onions, peppers and garlic in frying pan and cook until tender.
8. Pour in the eggs and cook for a further 3 minutes.
9. Turn out on to a hot dish.
10. Cut into two portions and surround with small pieces of toast spread with garlic-flavoured butter.

COUNTRY OMELETTE
(Illustrated on page 17)
Serves 2

1 potato, cooked
1 onion
2 tomatoes
2 tablespoons olive oil
shake of cayenne pepper
1 tablespoon tarragon vinegar
3 eggs
3 teaspoons water
salt and pepper

1. Peel and slice the potato. Skin and slice the onion and tomatoes.
2. Cook slowly in half the oil until tender but not browned.
3. Season with cayenne pepper and tarragon vinegar. Heat through well.
4. Beat the eggs lightly in a bowl, add the water and season well.
5. Add the potato mixture. Heat the remaining oil in a 9-inch (23cm) omelette pan. Pour in the egg mixture and cook, shaking the pan every so often.
6. Turn the omelette over when it is brown on one side.
7. Serve immediately, cut in half.

FAMILY CHEESE OMELETTE
Serves 4

6 eggs
3 tablespoons water
salt and pepper
1½oz (37gm) butter
6oz (150gm) Cheddar cheese, grated

1. Beat eggs with water and seasoning.
2. Melt butter in a large frying pan until hot, and pour in egg mixture.
3. Cook quickly, drawing outside mixture towards centre with a fork until the underside is golden brown and top still slightly soft.
4. Add cheese, fold in half and serve immediately.
5. Cut into four and serve with salad and potato crisps.

PEASANT OMELETTE
Serves 2

1oz (25gm) butter
2oz (50gm) raw pork, finely diced
2 potatoes, cooked and diced
1 teaspoon finely chopped parsley
1 teaspoon finely chopped chives
salt and freshly ground black pepper to taste
4 eggs

1. Melt butter in omelette pan and add pork.
2. When meat is browned remove to a plate and keep warm.
3. Add potatoes to the pan and fry until they are soft and golden.
4. Return pork to pan and add parsley, chives, salt and pepper.
5. Lightly beat eggs and pour into pan. Stir lightly then leave to set. Turn over and brown.
6. Slide out on to a plate and cut into two portions.

BAKED EGGS WITH YELLOW RICE
Serves 4

2½oz (62gm) butter
1 onion, chopped
½ teaspoon turmeric
8oz (200gm) long-grain rice
salt and pepper
boiling stock or water
4 large tomatoes
4 eggs

1. Preheat oven to moderately hot, 400 deg F or gas 6 (200 deg C).
2. Melt 2oz (50gm) butter in a pan and fry the onion lightly.
3. Add the turmeric, washed rice and salt and pepper.
4. Stir and cook the rice for about 5 minutes.
5. Add enough boiling stock or water to come about 1 inch above the rice in the pan.
6. Cook gently, stirring occasionally, until the rice is cooked and has absorbed the liquid.
7. Meanwhile, scoop out the inside of tomatoes, season and put a little butter in each.
8. Break an egg into each tomato and stand them in a baking tin.
9. Put a little more butter on the eggs.
10. Bake until the eggs are just set.
11. Dish up on a hot platter with the yellow rice. Serve with green beans.

EGGS IN HEAVEN
Serves 4

4oz (100gm) cooked gammon, minced
1 carton (8oz or 200gm) cottage cheese
4 eggs
salt and pepper
¼ pint (250ml) soured cream or natural yogurt

1. Preheat oven to moderate to moderately hot, 375 deg F or gas 5 (190 deg C).
2. Grease a shallow casserole and spoon in the gammon.
3. Top with cottage cheese and spoon four hollows out of the cheese. Break an egg into each.
4. Sprinkle with salt and pepper and pour over the cream over.
5. Bake on centre shelf of oven for 20 minutes.
6. Serve with baked tomatoes and a green vegetable.

EGGS IN A BLANKET
Serves 2

4 eggs
1oz (25gm) butter
1oz (25gm) flour
½ pint (250ml) milk
1½oz (37gm) cheese, grated
salt and pepper

1. Boil eggs for 4 minutes only. Shell the eggs carefully and keep them hot.
2. Melt the butter in a pan and stir in the flour.
3. Cook for a few minutes, stir well, but do not allow to brown.
4. Gradually add the milk, then bring to boil.
5. Add cheese and seasoning and simmer gently for 2 minutes.
6. Arrange the hot, shelled eggs in a dish, pour over the sauce and serve with grilled tomatoes and pieces of hot, buttered toast.

GOLDEN BAKED EGGS
Serves 4

shortcrust pastry made with
8oz (200gm) flour (see Basic
recipes, page 100)
4 hard-boiled eggs, shelled
1 teaspoon chopped parsley
grated rind of 1 lemon
salt and pepper
3 tablespoons milk
1oz (25gm) cheese, grated

1. Preheat oven to moderately
hot, 400 deg F or gas 6 (200 deg C).
2. Roll out pastry thinly and cut
into eight rounds.
3. Place 1 egg on each piece of
pastry. Sprinkle with parsley,
lemon rind and seasoning.
4. Damp the edges and cover with
a second round of pastry. Seal
well and neaten the edges.
5. Brush with milk and sprinkle
with cheese. Bake in centre of
oven for 20 minutes or until
golden.
6. Serve with a mixed salad.

EGG LOAF
Serves 2

1 small French loaf
4 hard-boiled eggs
1 stick celery
3 tomatoes, skinned
½ onion
2oz (50gm) butter, melted
salt and pepper

1. Preheat oven to moderate, 350
deg F or gas 4 (180 deg C).
2. Slice top off loaf, lengthways.
Remove soft centre, leaving a
shell.
3. Chop eggs, celery and
tomatoes.
4. Rub onion round inside of loaf,
then brush it with half the butter.
5. Add salt and pepper to egg
mixture. Spoon into loaf and
replace the top. Brush with rest of
butter.
6. Wrap in greaseproof paper and
bake for 20 minutes.
7. Cut the loaf in two and serve at
once.

EGGS WITH LIVER AND ONIONS
Serves 4

1lb (½ kilo) onions
2oz (50gm) butter
4oz (100gm) lamb's liver
salt and pepper
4oz (100gm) streaky bacon
rashers
8 eggs

1. Peel and slice onions thinly.
2. Cook gently, without
browning, in the butter.
3. Cut liver into small pieces, add
to the onion and sprinkle with
salt and pepper.
4. Increase the heat and cook for
about 5 minutes until liver is
tender.
5. Lift liver and onions out of pan
on to a heated serving plate and
keep hot.
6. Remove rinds and cut bacon
rashers into pieces.
7. Fry quickly in the same pan.
Lift out and keep hot.
8. Fry the eggs, put on top of the
liver and onions, and surround
with the bacon.
9. Serve hot with creamed potato
and carrots.

EGGS COUNTRY STYLE
Serves 4

1 packet bread sauce mix
½ pint (250ml) milk
4 large tomatoes
8oz (200gm) mushrooms
2oz (50gm) butter
salt and pepper
paprika
4 hard-boiled eggs
6oz (150gm) cheese, grated

1. Prepare bread sauce following
directions on the packet, using
milk.
2. Skin and slice tomatoes.
3. Quarter mushrooms.
4. Heat butter and gently cook
tomatoes and mushrooms. Season
with salt, pepper and paprika.
5. Halve eggs and place in a
shallow, ovenware serving dish.
Add mushrooms and tomatoes.
6. Stir half the cheese into
prepared sauce and pour over the
dish.
7. Top with remaining cheese and
place under a hot grill till top is
browned.

DUCHESSE EGG NESTS
(Illustrated on page 17)
Serves 4

1lb (½ kilo) mashed potato
1oz (25gm) plain flour
3 eggs, beaten
salt and pepper
2 tablespoons milk
¾oz (18gm) butter
1oz (25gm) cheese, grated

1. Preheat oven to moderate, 350
deg F or gas 4 (180 deg C).
2. Shape the potato into four flat
cakes and flour each lightly. Set
them in a greased baking tin.
3. Hollow out the centres with a
spoon.
4. Brush with a little beaten egg.
5. Bake for 15 minutes in centre
of oven until golden and set.
6. Season the rest of the eggs,
then add the milk.
7. Melt the butter in a saucepan
and add the rest of the eggs.
8. Cook slowly, stirring, until set.
9. Pile into the potato nests.
10. Sprinkle with cheese and
serve at once.

TOMATO AND CHEESE MIX
Serves 4

1oz (25gm) butter
1 onion, finely chopped
6oz (150gm) cheese, grated
6oz (150gm) breadcrumbs
1 small tomato, sliced
salt and pepper

1. Preheat oven to moderately
hot, 400 deg F or gas 6 (200 deg C).
2. Melt the butter in a pan and
cook onion until tender but not
brown.
3. Stir in cheese and breadcrumbs.
4. Spread in the bottom of a pie
dish.
5. Fill up the pie dish with layers
of the cheese mixture and
tomato slices.
6. Sprinkle with salt and pepper.
7. Bake in centre of oven for 15
minutes.

SAVOURY EGG PIE
Serves 4

3 slices white or brown bread
1 can oxtail soup
8 eggs
3oz (75gm) cheese, grated
2oz (50gm) salted peanuts

1. Preheat oven to moderate to moderately hot, 375 deg F or gas 5 (190 deg C).
2. Remove crusts and cut bread into small cubes.
3. Put into a basin and mix in the soup.
4. Hard-boil the eggs, then shell and chop them.
5. Add eggs and cheese to bread and soup mixture. Put into a buttered pie dish.
6. Chop peanuts finely and spread over the pie.
7. Bake for 25–30 minutes.
8. Serve hot with Brussels sprouts and parsnips.

POACHED EGGS WITH CHICKEN SAUCE
Serves 4

1 small Savoy cabbage
1 medium can condensed cream of chicken soup
1–2 tablespoons tomato ketchup
¼ teaspoon made mustard
pepper
8 eggs
1 teaspoon chopped parsley

1. Shred the cabbage finely, then wash and cook in boiling, salted water.
2. Mix soup with ketchup and mustard in a saucepan. Heat gently.
3. Drain cabbage well, mix in pepper to taste and spread in a buttered dish and keep hot.
4. Poach the eggs, drain on kitchen paper and arrange on top of the cabbage.
5. Pour sauce over the eggs. Sprinkle with parsley and serve hot.

EGGS IN CHEESE SAUCE
Serves 2

4 hot, hard-boiled eggs
1oz (25gm) butter
1oz (25gm) flour
½ pint (250ml) milk
salt and pepper
2oz (50gm) Cheddar cheese, grated

1. Slice the eggs into a buttered pie dish.
2. Melt the butter in a small pan.
3. Add the flour and cook for 2 minutes.
4. Remove from the heat and gradually beat in the milk.
5. Cook over a moderate heat until mixture thickens.
6. Season well and add most of the cheese.
7. Pour over the eggs in the pie dish.
8. Sprinkle with the remaining cheese and brown under a hot grill.

EGGS BENEDICT
Serves 4

4 slices bread
4 slices cooked ham
1oz (25gm) butter
1oz (25gm) flour
½ pint (250ml) milk
3oz (75gm) cheese, grated
salt and pepper
4 eggs
parsley or watercress to garnish

1. Toast one side of each slice of bread. Cover the other side with ham and grill slowly.
2. Melt butter in a saucepan, add flour and stir for 2–3 minutes.
3. Remove from heat and gradually add milk.
4. Return pan to heat and bring to boil, stirring all the time.
5. Add cheese and season to taste.
6. Remove from heat, stir until cheese has melted and cover with a lid.
7. Meanwhile, poach eggs and place one on top of each slice of ham.
9. Reheat sauce and pour it over the eggs.
10. Garnish with parsley or watercress.

EGG AND MUSHROOM AU GRATIN
Serves 4

4oz (100gm) mushrooms
2 tablespoons oil
4 eggs
1 packet (½ pint or 250ml) mushroom sauce mix
½ pint (250ml) milk
2oz (50gm) cheese, grated
few breadcrumbs

1. Slice the mushrooms and fry in the oil. Put into an ovenware dish.
2. Poach the eggs and put on top of the mushrooms.
3. Make up the sauce as directed on the packet using the milk.
4. Add most of the cheese and pour sauce over the eggs.
5. Sprinkle the rest of the cheese and the breadcrumbs on top and brown under the grill.

EGG AND HAM CROQUETTES
Serves 4

2 hard-boiled eggs, chopped
4oz (100gm) ham, chopped
¼ pint (125ml) thick white sauce (see Basic recipes, page 100)
salt and pepper
flour
1 egg, beaten
breadcrumbs
fat for frying

1. Mix eggs and ham into white sauce and season to taste.
2. Leave to cool, then form into eight sausage-shaped croquettes.
3. Dip in flour and egg, then coat with breadcrumbs.
4. Deep fry until golden brown.
5. Drain and serve the croquettes with grilled tomatoes.

EGG AND TOMATO SUPPER
Serves 4

6 eggs
salt and pepper
1 tablespoon milk
8oz (200gm) tomatoes, sliced
small piece onion
a little chopped parsley
2 tablespoons stock
1oz (25gm) butter

1. Break the eggs into a bowl, season with salt and pepper and beat in the milk.
2. Put the tomatoes into a pan.
3. Chop the onion very finely and add to the tomatoes with the parsley.
4. Add the stock and simmer very slowly until the tomatoes are tender.
5. Sieve into a fresh pan and boil to a thick, sauce-like consistency.
6. Melt the butter in a pan; pour in the eggs and stir gently until set.
7. Spoon them on to a hot serving plate in a ring and fill the centre with the tomato mixture.
8. Serve piping hot.

PORTUGUESE EGGS
Serves 4

4 tomatoes
3oz (75gm) butter
2 onions
4 eggs
salt and pepper
8 rounds buttered toast
parsley to garnish

1. Skin and halve the tomatoes.
2. Top with a little of the butter and grill. Put on a plate and keep hot.
3. Slice the onions, then fry in hot fat.
3. Scramble the eggs with the rest of the butter. Season and pile on top of the tomatoes.
4. Put some onion rings on top and serve hot on the toast. Garnish with parsley.

CHEESE AND RICE LOAF WITH MUSHROOM SAUCE
Serves 4

2oz (50gm) butter
scant ½ pint (scant 250ml) milk
4oz (100gm) cooked long-grain rice (raw weight)
6oz (150gm) cheese, grated
1½oz (37gm) fresh breadcrumbs
3 eggs, lightly beaten
4oz (100gm) celery, finely chopped
2oz (50gm) onion, minced
1 teaspoon chopped parsley
4oz (100gm) green pepper, chopped
1 teaspoon salt
½ teaspoon prepared mustard
1 can condensed cream of mushroom soup
¼ pint (125ml) water
1 can (3–4oz or 75–100gm) mushrooms, sliced

1. Preheat oven to moderate, 350 deg F or gas 4 (180 deg C).
2. Heat butter in a pan with milk until butter has melted.
3. Mix rice, cheese and crumbs with eggs; stir into hot milk.
4. Add celery, onion, parsley, green pepper and seasonings.
5. Turn into a greased and lined loaf tin.
6. Bake for 1¼ hours.
7. Turn out on to a serving dish.
8. Blend soup with water until smooth, then add mushrooms.
9. Heat through and serve with the rice loaf.

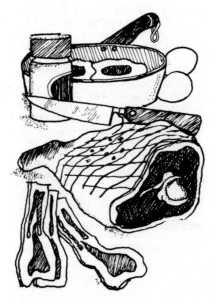

CRUSTY CHEESE BAKE
Serves 4

8 slices bread buttered
6oz (150gm) cheese, grated
4oz (100gm) mushrooms
4oz (100gm) ham, chopped
4 eggs
pinch of dry mustard
1½ pints (approximately ¾ litre) milk

1. Preheat oven to moderate to moderately hot, 375 deg F or gas 5 (190 deg C).
2. Cut each slice of bread into four pieces.
3. Fill a greased ovenware dish with layers of bread, cheese (reserving about one third for the top), sliced mushrooms and ham.
4. Finish with a layer of bread.
5. Sprinkle with the rest of the cheese.
6. Beat eggs with mustard and milk and pour over bread.
7. Bake on centre shelf of oven for 45 minutes, until set and golden.

HOT CHEESE PUFF
Serves 4

3oz (75gm) butter
2oz (50gm) flour
½ pint (250ml) milk
4 eggs, separated
4oz (100gm) cheese, grated
salt and cayenne pepper

1. Preheat oven to moderately hot, 400 deg F or gas 6 (200 deg C).
2. Grease a 2-pint (approximately 1 litre) soufflé dish or deep casserole.
3. Melt the butter in a pan.
4. Add the flour and cook for a moment without browning.
5. Remove from heat and gradually beat in the milk.
6. Return to the heat and cook until thickened.
7. Beat the egg yolks into the hot mixture.
8. Add all but 1 tablespoon cheese. Season.
9. Whisk egg whites until stiff.
10. Fold them gently into the cheese mixture.
11. Turn into the prepared soufflé dish and sprinkle with the remaining cheese.
12. Bake in centre of oven until well risen.
13. Remove from oven and serve immediately.

CHEESE FLUFF
Serves 2

2 eggs
½ pint (250ml) warm milk
3oz (75gm) cheese, grated
¼ level teaspoon mustard
2 level teaspoons chopped
parsley
1 level teaspoon salt
2oz (50gm) breadcrumbs

1. Preheat oven to moderately
hot, 400 deg F or gas 6 (200 deg C).
2. Grease a 2-pint (approximately
1 litre) casserole.
3. Separate eggs and blend yolks
with milk, cheese and mustard.
4. Add parsley and salt.
5. Pour over the breadcrumbs and
leave to get cold.
6. Whisk egg whites until stiff
and fold into the breadcrumb
mixture.
7. Pour into the casserole and
bake in centre of oven for 30
minutes. Serve at once.

SAVOURY CHEESE AND NUTS
Serves 4

1½lb (¾ kilo) cooked vegetables
1oz (25gm) lard
1oz (25gm) flour
½ pint (250ml) milk
½ green pepper, chopped
½oz (12gm) nuts, chopped
salt and pepper
2oz (50gm) cheese, grated

1. Places vegetables in a fireproof
dish.
2. Melt fat in a strong pan and
stir in flour.
3. Remove from heat and
gradually add milk, stirring until
the mixture is smooth.
4. Still stirring, return to heat
and bring to boil. (The sauce
should be of a coating
consistency.)
5. Add green pepper and nuts,
season well and pour over
vegetables.
6. Sprinkle with cheese and grill
until golden brown and heated
through.

CHEESE AND HAM PIE
Serves 4

Layers of bread, mushrooms,
cheese and ham baked in the oven.

5 slices bread
2oz (50gm) mushrooms
2oz (50gm) cheese, grated
2oz (50gm) ham
4 eggs
1 level teaspoon dry mustard
1 pint (approximately ½ litre)
milk

1. Preheat oven to moderate to
moderately hot, 375 deg F or gas 5
(190 deg C).
2. Trim the crusts off the bread
and cut each slice into four or
five pieces.
3. Slice the mushrooms.
4. Fill an ovenware dish with
layers of bread, mushrooms,
cheese and ham, finishing with a
layer of cheese.
5. Beat eggs and mustard into the
milk and pour over the layers.
6. Bake in centre of oven for 45
minutes.

GOLDEN CHEESE PIE
Serves 4

1 egg
1lb (½ kilo) mashed potato
6oz (150gm) cheese, grated
1 onion, finely chopped
½oz (12gm) lard
2 tomatoes

1. Preheat oven to moderately
hot, 400 deg F or gas 6 (200 deg C).
2. Beat egg into potatoes with 4oz
(100gm) cheese.
3. Fry onion in the lard until
tender, then add to potatoes.
4. Turn into a buttered pie dish
and sprinkle with the rest of the
cheese.
5. Slice tomatoes, arrange over
top and cover with a piece of foil.
6. Bake in centre of oven for 25
minutes.

MACNAMARA PIE
Serves 4

2oz (50gm) butter
2 small onions, sliced
1lb (½ kilo) potatoes, thinly
sliced
½ packet powdered tomato soup
3 small portions Gruyère
processed cheese, sieved
1 egg
¼ pint (125ml) milk
salt and pepper

1. Preheat oven to moderately
hot, 400 deg F or gas 6 (200 deg C).
2. Melt 1oz (25gm) butter in a
saucepan and fry the onions until
tender.
3. Grease a fireproof dish and
place a layer of potatoes in the
bottom.
4. Sprinkle some of the powdered
tomato soup on top, then add
some onion and some cheese.
5. Continue adding layers until
all the ingredients are used up,
finishing with a layer of potato.
6. Beat the egg into the milk,
season and pour over the potato.
7. Dot with the rest of the butter.
8. Bake in centre of oven for 1
hour until crisp and golden on
top.

CHEESE BAKE
Serves 4

4 large potatoes
1 onion
2 carrots
1 tablespoon chopped parsley
salt and pepper
6 bacon rashers, chopped
4oz (100gm) cheese
¾ pint (375ml) milk

1. Preheat oven to moderate to moderately hot, 375 deg F or gas 5 (190 deg C).
2. Peel and slice the potatoes.
3. Peel and slice the onion and the carrots.
4. Put a layer of potato into the bottom of a pie dish and add some of the onion and carrot.
5. Sprinkle with parsley and salt and pepper.
6. Add a layer of bacon.
7. Build up the pie dish in layers until it is full.
8. Top with the thinly sliced cheese.
9. Pour the milk over.
10. Bake for 1 hour in centre of oven.

CHEESE PANCAKES
Serves 4

4oz (100gm) plain flour
1 egg
½ pint (250ml) milk
4oz (100gm) cheese, grated
salt and pepper
1oz (25gm) lard

1. Sift the flour into a bowl and break in the egg.
2. Add the milk and 3 oz (75gm) cheese and mix to a smooth batter. Season well.
3. Melt a little of the lard in the frying pan.
4. Pour in a little of the batter and make pancakes in the usual way.
5. Pile on to a hot plate, sprinkle with remaining cheese and grill under a hot grill until a golden brown.
6. Serve at once with hot sausages.

PIQUANT CHEESE DREAMS
Serves 4

8 slices bread
butter
chutney
4oz (100gm) cheese, grated
2oz (50gm) dripping
parsley to garnish

1. Spread the bread with butter and chutney.
2. Sprinkle liberally with cheese.
3. Make four whole sandwiches.
4. Melt the dripping and fry the sandwiches until brown and crisp on both sides.
5. Serve hot garnished with parsley. Accompany with tomato sauce.

CHEESE AND POTATO PUFFS
Serves 4

1½lb (¾ kilo) potatoes
½oz (12gm) butter
¼ teaspoon prepared mustard
3oz (75gm) cheese, grated
salt and pepper
1 egg, beaten
2oz (50gm) breadcrumbs
fat for frying

1. Boil the potatoes and mash them while still hot, adding butter, mustard, cheese, seasoning and sufficient egg to bind.
2. Shape the mixture into balls.
3. Brush with rest of egg and roll balls in breadcrumbs.
4. Fry in hot fat until golden brown. Drain.
5. Serve with a mixed salad.

POTATO CHEESE CRISP
Serves 4

1lb (½ kilo) onions
2lb (1 kilo) potatoes
2oz (50gm) dripping
8oz (200gm) Cheddar cheese, grated
salt and pepper
1 pint (approximately ½ litre) chicken stock

1. Preheat oven to moderate to moderately hot, 375 deg F or gas 5 (190 deg C).
2. Skin the onions.
3. Peel the potatoes and dry them well in a cloth.
4. Heat half the dripping in a fireproof casserole and add a layer of sliced potatoes, a layer of cheese and then one of onions, seasoning each layer well.
5. Cook gently over a low heat for 2 minutes.
6. Top with rest of dripping.
7. Add the hot stock. Cover with a lid.
8. Transfer to the centre shelf of oven for 30 minutes, or until potato is cooked.

SWISS CHEESE PLATTER
Serves 4

8 bacon rashers
2oz (50gm) Gruyère or Emmenthal cheese
4 eggs
¼ pint (125ml) cream
salt and pepper

1. Preheat oven to moderate, 350 deg F or gas 4 (180 deg C).
2. Lightly grill the bacon.
3. Butter a warmed pie dish well. Line with bacon rashers.
4. Slice the cheese as thinly as possible and scatter over the bacon.
5. Break in the eggs and pour the cream over.
6. Bake in centre of oven for about 6 minutes or until the eggs are very nearly set.
7. Remove from the oven. The heat remaining in the dish will set the eggs firmly.

WELSH RAREBIT
Serves 4

1½oz (37gm) butter
1½oz (37gm) flour
½ pint (250ml) milk
a little made mustard
salt and pepper
3oz (75gm) cheese, grated
4 rounds buttered toast

1. Melt the butter, stir in the flour and cook without browning.
2. Remove from heat and stir in the milk gradually, until smooth. Return to the heat and cook, stirring, for 1–2 minutes.
3. Add a little made mustard, salt and pepper and the cheese.
4. Spread on to hot buttered toast and put under a hot grill until golden brown.
5. Serve with grilled tomatoes.

CHEESE AND PINEAPPLE FLAN
Serves 4

cheese pastry made with 4oz (100gm) flour (see Basic recipes, page 100)
3oz (75gm) Cheddar cheese, grated
1 small can pineapple rings
radishes
1 teaspoon Worcestershire sauce
2 level teaspoons arrowroot

1. Preheat oven to hot, 425 deg F or gas 7 (220 deg C).
2. Roll pastry out thinly and line a 7-inch (18cm) flan ring. Prick base, line with greaseproof paper and fill with dried beans.
3. Bake in centre of oven for 25 minutes, removing beans and paper after 15 minutes cooking. Leave to cool.
4. Spread cheese in cooled flan case and arrange drained pineapple rings on top.
5. Place a radish flower in the centre of each ring.
6. Make Worcestershire sauce up to ¼ pint (125ml) with pineapple juice. Blend the arrowroot with liquid and bring to the boil, stirring constantly. Continue to cook until mixture has thickened.
7. Pour over flan and allow to set.
8. Chill and serve with salad.

QUICHE LORRAINE
(Illustrated on page 17)
Serves 6

shortcrust pastry made with 8oz (200gm) flour (see Basic recipes, page 100)
5 eggs
6oz (150gm) cheese, grated
salt and pepper
1½oz (37gm) butter, melted
1 pint (approximately ½ litre) creamy milk
1 small onion, finely chopped and lightly fried
4oz (100gm) streaky bacon, chopped
sprig of parsley

1. Preheat oven to moderately hot, 400 deg F or gas 6 (200 deg C).
2. Line a 12-inch (30cm) flan tin with pastry and prick the base.
3. Break the eggs into a bowl and add the cheese, seasoning and butter.
4. Whisk in the milk and add the onion and the bacon.
5. Pour into the pastry case and bake in centre of oven for approximately 40 minutes or until filling is puffy and golden brown.
6. Serve hot or cold garnished with a sprig of parsley.

CHEESE AND LEEK PIE
Serves 4

shortcrust pastry made with 6oz (150gm) flour (see Basic recipes, page 100)
3 leeks, parboiled
1oz (25gm) flour, seasoned with salt and pepper
4oz (100gm) cheese, grated
2 tablespoons top of the milk
1 egg, beaten

1. Preheat oven to moderately hot, 400 deg F or gas 6 (200 deg C).
2. Line a pie plate with 4oz (100gm) pastry.
3. Cut the leeks into rounds. Put them on the pastry and sprinkle with a little seasoned flour.
4. Cover with cheese and add the milk.
5. Roll out the rest of the pastry. Cut into strips and twist these lattice fashion over the top. Brush with egg.
6. Bake in centre of oven for about 30 minutes.

FRENCH FLAN
Serves 4–6

shortcrust pastry made with 6oz (150gm) flour (see Basic recipes, page 100)
1oz (25gm) butter
1lb (½ kilo) onions, thinly sliced
2 tablespoons Worcestershire sauce
1 teaspoon tomato purée
salt and pepper
6oz (150gm) cooked ham, thinly sliced
6oz (150gm) Cheddar cheese, grated
2 tomatoes, sliced
sprig of parsley

1. Preheat oven to moderately hot, 400 deg F or gas 6 (200 deg C).
2. Roll pastry out thinly and use to line a 7-inch (18cm) square, shallow baking tin.
3. Prick the base, line with foil and fill with baking beans. Bake in centre of oven for 15 minutes.
4. Remove foil and beans and bake for a further 5 minutes.
5. Melt butter in pan and fry onions very gently for 5 minutes, stirring occasionally.
6. Add Worcestershire sauce, tomato purée and seasoning.
7. Layer the onion, ham and cheese in the flan case, finishing with a layer of cheese.
8. Return to oven for 15 minutes or until cheese has just melted.
9. Arrange tomatoes round edge of flan and put parsley in centre. Serve hot or cold with vegetables or a salad.

CHEESE TARTLETS
Makes 12

shortcrust pastry made with
3oz (75gm) flour (see Basic
recipes, page 100)
½ teaspoon anchovy paste
1 egg, separated
½oz (12gm) butter
1 level teaspoon cornflour
4 tablespoons milk
1oz (25gm) Cheddar cheese,
grated
salt and cayenne pepper
paprika pepper

1. Preheat oven to moderately
hot, 400 deg F or gas 6 (200 deg C).
2. Roll out pastry and line 12
small patty tins. Put a dash of
anchovy paste in each.
3. Beat egg yolk. Heat butter in a
pan, stir in cornflour and remove
from heat.
4. Gradually blend in the milk
and egg yolk. Stir in the cheese
and salt and pepper.
5. Whisk egg white until stiff and
fold into cheese mixture.
6. Spoon into the pastry cases,
filling them only three-quarters
full.
7. Bake on second shelf down of
oven for 20 minutes.
8. Serve piping hot sprinkled with
paprika pepper.

COTTAGE CHEESE TART
Serves 4

shortcrust pastry made with
6oz (150gm) flour (see Basic
recipes, page 100)
1 large onion
½oz (12gm) butter
1 tablespoon capers
2 eggs
¼ pint (125ml) cream or top of
the milk
8oz (200gm) cottage cheese
salt and pepper
8 anchovy fillets

1. Preheat oven to moderately
hot, 400 deg F or gas 6 (200 deg C).
2. Roll out the pastry and line an
8-inch (20cm) flan tin or sandwich
cake tin.
3. Prick the base, line with foil
and fill with dried haricot beans.
4. Bake on centre shelf of oven for
10 minutes, then remove beans
and bake for a further 5 minutes.
5. Turn oven down to moderate,
350 deg F or gas 4 (180 deg C).
6. Chop onion finely and fry in
butter until golden brown.
7. Add chopped capers, beaten
eggs, cream or milk and cottage
cheese.
8. Season and turn into the hot
flan case and garnish with a
lattice of anchovy fillets.
9. Bake on centre shelf of oven
until filling is set.

CHEESE AND TOMATO PATTIES
Serves 4

shortcrust pastry made with
6oz (150gm) flour (see Basic
recipes, page 100)
3oz (75gm) mushrooms
4oz (100gm) cheese, thinly
sliced
4 eggs
salt and cayenne pepper
¾ pint (375ml) single cream
or milk
1oz (25gm) butter, melted
tomatoes
watercress

1. Preheat oven to moderately
hot, 400 deg F or gas 6 (200 deg C).
2. Line some patty tins with the
pastry.
3. Fry the sliced mushrooms and
put a few into each patty case.
Cover with a slice of cheese.
4. Beat the eggs with seasoning,
cream or milk and butter and
pour a little into each pastry case.
5. Put a slice of tomato on top.
6. Bake for 40 minutes, until set
and golden.
7. Garnish with watercress.

CHEESE NIBBLES
Serves 4

2 large potatoes
2oz (50gm) self-raising flour
4oz (100gm) cheese, grated
2 eggs, beaten
salt and pepper
fat for frying

1. Grate the potato finely and
drain.
2. Mix in all the other
ingredients with salt and pepper
to taste.
3. Fry small spoonfuls of the
mixture in hot fat.
4. Drain on absorbent paper and
serve hot, with salad or a green
vegetable.

Pasta

There is nothing more appetising than a plate of spaghetti. Never cook pasta before you are ready to serve it, as it does not keep hot to advantage.

SPAGHETTI RAREBIT
(Illustrated on page 17)
Serves 4

3oz (75gm) spaghetti
1oz (25gm) butter
¼ pint (125ml) beer
pinch paprika pepper
pinch cayenne pepper
¼ teaspoon dry mustard
1½ teaspoons piquant table sauce
8oz (200gm) cheese, grated
4 slices bread, toasted

1. Cook the spaghetti in boiling salted water for 15 minutes, until just tender.
2. Drain and toss in the butter.
3. Place in a hot serving dish and keep warm.
4. Pour the beer into a pan, add the seasonings and heat gently.
5. When hot, add the cheese and stir until melted.
6. Pour over the spaghetti.
7. Place spaghetti on toast, then grill until cheese browns slightly.

MEAT BALLS WITH SPAGHETTI
Serves 4

1lb (½ kilo) lean beef, minced
1 egg
1 onion, finely chopped
salt and pepper
2oz (50gm) flour plus a little extra
2oz (50gm) butter
½ pint (250ml) tomato juice
1 bayleaf
8oz (200gm) spaghetti
grated Parmesan or Cheddar cheese

1. Mix together the minced beef, egg and onion.
2. Season well. Form into small balls.
3. Flour lightly with additional flour.
4. Fry in some of the butter until they are cooked and browned.
5. Remove and keep hot.
6. Put remaining fat into a saucepan, add the 2oz (50gm) flour and cook over a low heat for a minute.
7. Stir in the tomato juice gradually, and add bayleaf.
8. Bring to the boil and simmer for 7 minutes.
9. Adjust seasoning, place meat balls in the sauce and simmer a few minutes more.
10. Cook spaghetti in a large pan of boiling, salted water for 15 minutes. Drain.
11. Arrange the meat balls on the piping hot spaghetti, cover with sauce and serve with grated cheese.

SPAGHETTI NAPOLITANA
Serves 4

2 medium onions, chopped
2 tablespoons olive oil
1 large can tomatoes, or
1lb (½ kilo) fresh ones, chopped
1 garlic clove, crushed
sprig of rosemary
1 teaspoon sugar
salt and pepper
pinch of cayenne pepper
1lb (½ kilo) spaghetti
Parmesan cheese

1. Fry the onions in the oil, until transparent but not browned.
2. Add tomatoes, garlic, rosemary, sugar, salt and pepper and cayenne pepper.
3. Bring to the boil and simmer for at least 30 minutes.
4. While the sauce is cooking, cook the spaghetti in a large pan of boiling, salted water for 15 minutes or until tender.
5. Rub sauce through a sieve, or liquidise in an electric blender for a few moments.
6. Reheat the sauce and pour over the hot spaghetti.
7. Serve with Parmesan cheese.

SPAGHETTI LUNCH DISH
Serves 6

4 tablespoons butter
1 onion, chopped
1 green pepper, chopped
1lb (½ kilo) minced beef
1 medium can tomatoes
1½ teaspoons salt
½ teaspoon pepper
12oz (300gm) Cheddar or Swiss
cheese, cubed
1lb (½ kilo) spaghetti
1½oz (37gm) Cheddar, Gruyère
or Parmesan cheese, grated

1. Melt the butter in a large
saucepan.
2. Add onion and green pepper
and fry for 5 minutes.
3. Add the beef and cook over a
high heat, stirring constantly
until brown.
4. Add the tomatoes, salt and
pepper.
5. Cover and cook over a low
heat for 1 hour.
6. Add the cubed cheese and cook
for 5 minutes.
7. Meanwhile, cook the spaghetti
in a large pan of boiling, salted
water for 15 minutes. Drain then
add it to the sauce. Mix
thoroughly but lightly.
8. Serve with grated cheese.

SPAGHETTI SCRAMBLE
Serves 4

1 small packet quick-dried peas
8oz (200gm) spaghetti
4 large tomatoes, skinned
4oz (100gm) corned beef, diced
12oz (300gm) Cheddar cheese,
grated
1oz (25gm) butter
salt and pepper

1. Cook peas as directed on
packet.
2. Cook the spaghetti in a large
pan of boiling, salted water until
tender.
3. Cut tomatoes into slices.
4. Mix drained peas and the
corned beef into drained
spaghetti. Add tomatoes, cheese
and butter.
5. Heat gently for a few minutes,
stirring once or twice only.
6. Season and serve at once.

SPAGHETTI MOUSSAKA
Serves 4

2 large aubergines
3 medium onions, roughly
chopped
2oz (50gm) butter
1lb (½ kilo) minced beef
8oz (200gm) tomatoes, peeled
and quartered
salt and pepper
1 medium can spaghetti hoops
2oz (50gm) breadcrumbs
2oz (50gm) cheese, grated

1. Preheat oven to moderate, 350
deg F or gas 4 (180 deg C).
2. Wash and slice aubergines; salt
heavily.
3. Place between two plates for as
long as possible to extract the
bitter juices.
4. Fry the onions in half the
butter until tender.
5. Add the minced beef and
tomatoes and cook for 5 minutes.
Season well.
6. Rinse and dry aubergines and
lightly fry in remaining butter.
7. Place half the meat mixture in
the bottom of a 2-pint
(approximately 1 litre) casserole
and arrange aubergines on top.
8. Cover with the rest of the meat
mixture.
9. Top with spaghetti hoops.
10. Mix breadcrumbs and cheese
together and sprinkle the mixture
into the centre of the spaghetti
hoops. Cover with a lid.
11. Bake in centre of oven for 1
hour.
12. Remove the lid for the last 15
minutes, to brown the
breadcrumbs and cheese topping.

QUICK PORK AND SPAGHETTI
Serves 4

1 onion, skinned
2 tablespoons chopped red
pepper
4oz (100gm) mushrooms,
chopped
2oz (50gm) butter
1 medium can tomatoes
1 teaspoon chopped sage
salt and pepper
1 can pork luncheon meat,
diced
10oz (250gm) spaghetti
2oz (50gm) Cheddar cheese,
grated

1. Grate onion, mix with pepper
and mushrooms and fry gently in
1oz (25gm) butter, for 5 minutes.
2. Add tomatoes, sage and
seasoning and simmer for about
20 minutes, until vegetables are
soft.
3. Add luncheon meat and cook
for a further 5 minutes to heat it
through.
4. Meanwhile, cook spaghetti in
a large saucepan of boiling, salted
water for 15 minutes.
5. Drain well and toss in the
remaining butter.
6. Arrange the spaghetti as a
border on a hot dish.
7. Pour the sauce into the centre
and sprinkle with cheese.

SAVOURY SPAGHETTI
Serves 4

1lb (½ kilo) onions
6oz (150gm) spaghetti
salt and pepper
4oz (100gm) cheese, grated
1½oz (37gm) butter

1. Preheat oven to very moderate,
325 deg F or gas 3 (170 deg C).
2. Boil the onions and chop them
roughly.
3. Meanwhile, cook the spaghetti
in plenty of boiling, salted water
for 15 minutes until tender, then
drain.
4. Place alternate layers of
spaghetti and onions in a pie dish.
5. Season, cover with cheese and
dot with butter.
6. Bake for 20 minutes and then
turn heat up and leave until
browned.

Duchesse egg nests (see page 8)   Country omelette (see page 6)

Quiche Lorraine (see page 13)   Spaghetti rarebit (see page 15)

Cold meat with macaroni salad (see page 19)   Noodles with meat sauce (see page 21)

Sugared ham with peaches and prunes (see page 25)   Bacon parcels with mushrooms and tomatoes (see page 22)

VENETIAN HAM
Serves 4

12oz (300gm) spaghetti
1½oz (37gm) butter
1 onion, chopped
1 packet (½ pint or 250ml)
mushroom sauce mix
½ pint (250ml) milk
1 small can tomatoes
12oz (300gm) cooked ham, diced
½ level teaspoon dried
marjoram
dash Worcestershire sauce

1. Cook the spaghetti in a pan of
boiling, salted water for 15
minutes. Drain and keep hot.
2. Melt the butter in a pan and
fry the onion gently until tender.
3. Stir in the sauce mix and the
milk.
4. Simmer for 2 minutes.
5. Stir in tomatoes, ham,
marjoram and Worcestershire
sauce.
6. Bring to the boil and simmer
for 15 minutes.
7. Pour sauce over the spaghetti.

MACARONI CHEESE
Serves 4

6oz (150gm) macaroni
1oz (25gm) butter
1oz (25gm) flour
¾ pint (375ml) milk
1 teaspoon Tabasco sauce
a little made mustard
salt
6oz (150gm) cheese, grated

1. Cook the macaroni in fast
boiling, salted water for 10
minutes. Drain and keep hot.
2. Melt the butter in a saucepan.
3. Stir in the flour and add the
milk.
4. Bring to the boil and add
Tabasco sauce, mustard and salt.
Simmer for 10 minutes.
5. Stir in 4oz (100gm) cheese.
6. Stir in the well-drained
macaroni and blend well.
7. Put the mixture into a pie dish
and sprinkle the top with
remaining cheese.
8. Brown under the grill, or in a
hot oven.

MACARONI CHEESE
SPECIAL
Serves 4

2 tablespoons chopped
red pepper
½oz (12gm) butter
1 large can evaporated milk
6oz (150gm) cheese, grated
2 teaspoons mustard
1 teaspoon piquant table sauce
3 tablespoons cooked peas
salt and pepper
6oz (150gm) macaroni

1. Fry the pepper in butter until
tender, then drain.
2. Mix with milk and 5oz (125gm)
cheese.
3. Bring slowly to the boil,
stirring, until cheese melts and
sauce thickens.
4. Mix in mustard, sauce and peas
and season to taste.
5. Cook macaroni in boiling,
salted water for 8–10 minutes,
then drain and add to sauce.
6. Pour into a heatproof dish and
sprinkle with the remaining
cheese.
7. Grill until bubbling and golden.

COLD MEAT WITH
MACARONI SALAD
(Illustrated on page 18)
Serves 4

8oz (200gm) macaroni
1 small packet frozen mixed
vegetables
1 tomato
1 green pepper
mayonnaise
salt and pepper
lemon juice
assorted cold meats

1. Cook the macaroni in boiling,
salted water until just tender.
2. Drain and rinse through with
cold water. Leave to get quite
cold.
3. Cook the frozen vegetables,
drain and add to the macaroni.
4. Cut the tomato into strips and
de-seed it.
5. Cut the green pepper into thin
strips about 1-inch long, taking
care to remove all seeds.
6. Add the tomato and pepper to
the macaroni mixture and moisten
with mayonnaise.
7. Season with salt and pepper
and a squeeze of lemon juice.
8. Arrange cold meats on a
serving dish and accompany with
small bowls of macaroni salad.

GOLDEN MACARONI BAKE
Serves 4

4oz (100gm) ham
4oz (100gm) cooked chicken
1 small can tomatoes
6oz (150gm) quick-cooking
macaroni
2½oz (62gm) butter
¾oz (18gm) flour
¾ pint (375ml) milk
salt and cayenne pepper
4oz (100gm) Parmesan cheese
fried mushrooms and parsley
to garnish

1. Preheat oven to moderately
hot, 400 deg F or gas 6 (200 deg C).
2. Shred the ham and chicken.
3. Drain and roughly chop the
tomatoes.
4. Cook the macaroni in plenty
of boiling, salted water, for 7
minutes, drain well and toss in 1oz
(25gm) of the butter.
5. Heat 1oz (25gm) of butter in a
pan, blend in the flour and cook
over a gentle heat for a minute.
6. Remove from the heat and
gradually beat in the milk.
7. Season well to taste and stir
until thickened, over the heat.
8. Mix in 3oz (75gm) cheese and
combine this sauce with the
macaroni, ham, chicken and
tomatoes.
9. Adjust seasoning and turn into
a 2-pint (approximately 1 litre) pie
dish.
10. Sprinkle with the rest of the
cheese and dabs of the remaining
butter.
11. Bake for 20 minutes.
12. Garnish with mushrooms and
parsley.

SAMARONI
Serves 4

6oz (150gm) macaroni
1 can (8oz or 200gm) tuna fish
or salmon
1 can mushroom soup
1 level tablespoon finely
chopped onion

1. Preheat oven to moderate, 350 deg F or gas 4 (180 deg C).
2. Cook the macaroni in plenty of boiling, salted water for about 10 minutes, or until just tender.
3. Drain and add the rest of the ingredients.
4. Turn into a buttered casserole dish, and dot with butter.
5. Bake for 30–45 minutes, or until bubbling and golden brown on top.
6. Serve with a crisp, green salad and hot rolls and butter.

MACARONI EGGS
Serves 4

6oz (150gm) quick-cooking
macaroni
1 can condensed tomato soup
⅓ can water or milk
2 medium onions
salt and pepper
3 hard-boiled eggs

1. Boil macaroni in a large pan of boiling, salted water for 7 minutes.
2. Drain, then add soup, water or milk and 1 finely chopped onion.
3. Season to taste.
4. Pour into a warmed serving dish.
5. Slice the hard-boiled eggs and onion. Fry onion in a little butter.
6. Garnish top with eggs and onion and serve at once.

DEVILLED EGG CASSEROLE
Serves 4

3 hard-boiled eggs
2 tablespoons mayonnaise
salt and pepper
¼ teaspoon made mustard
1 small can tomato soup
2 tablespoons water
½ tablespoon grated onion
1oz (25gm) cheese, grated
4oz (100gm) cooked macaroni
(raw weight)
1 can sardines

1. Preheat oven to moderate, 350 deg F or gas 4 (180 deg C).
2. Halve eggs lengthways. Remove yolks and mash with mayonnaise, salt, pepper and mustard.
3. Pile back into whites.
4. Combine soup, water, onion and half the cheese in a pan.
5. Cook gently until cheese melts, then combine with the macaroni.
6. Pour into a casserole. Sprinkle with remaining cheese and arrange eggs and sardines on top.
7. Cover and cook in oven for 35 minutes.

MACARONI BAKE
Serves 4

8oz (200gm) macaroni
2 tablespoons corn oil
4oz (100gm) mushrooms
1 packet (½ pint or 250ml)
cheese sauce mix
½ pint (250ml) milk
1 medium can tomatoes
1 medium can sweetcorn
1 medium can luncheon meat,
diced
grated Parmesan cheese

1. Cook the macaroni in boiling, salted water for 10–15 minutes until tender. Drain well.
2. Meanwhile, heat the corn oil and fry the mushrooms until tender.
3. Make up the cheese sauce as directed on the packet using milk.
4. Stir in the tomatoes, corn, luncheon meat and macaroni.
5. Reserve a few mushrooms for garnish and add the remainder to the macaroni mixture.
6. Heat through. Pile into a serving dish.
7. Garnish with mushroom slices and sprinkle with Parmesan cheese.

MACARONI AND CHEESE PLATTER
Serves 4

8oz (200gm) macaroni
3oz (75gm) Cheddar cheese,
cubed
1 onion, grated
3 bacon rashers, chopped
4 tomatoes, peeled and chopped
2oz (50gm) butter
salt
2 eggs, beaten
1 pint (approximately ½ litre)
milk
1oz (25gm) cheese, grated
1oz (25gm) breadcrumbs

1. Preheat oven to moderate, 350 deg F or gas 4 (180 deg C).
2. Cook the macaroni in boiling, salted water for about 10 minutes, then drain.
3. In a buttered ovenware dish, place alternate layers of macaroni, cheese, onion, bacon and tomatoes, dotting each layer with butter and sprinkling with salt.
4. Finish with a layer of macaroni.
5. Mix the eggs with milk and pour over the macaroni.
6. Sprinkle the top with grated cheese and breadcrumbs and bake for about 40 minutes.

MACARONI WITH ONIONS AND CHEESE
Serves 4

2 medium onions
6oz (150gm) macaroni
1 pint (approximately ½ litre)
white sauce (see Basic recipes,
page 100)
1 teaspoon made mustard
salt and cayenne pepper
4oz (100gm) cheese, grated

1. Skin the onions, cut into rings and cook with the macaroni in boiling, salted water for 10 minutes or until tender. Drain.
2. Add the onions and macaroni to the white sauce, then leave to cool slightly.
3. Add the seasonings and 2½oz (62gm) cheese.
4. Turn this mixture into a greased dish and sprinkle the remainder of the cheese on top.
5. Brown and heat through under a hot grill.

NOODLE SOUFFLE
Serves 4

6oz (150gm) noodles
1oz (25gm) butter
2oz (50gm) soft breadcrumbs
2oz (50gm) cheese, grated
4oz (100gm) ham or chicken,
chopped
¼ pint (125ml) top of the milk
salt and pepper
3 eggs, separated

1. Preheat oven to moderate, 350 deg F or gas 4 (180 deg C).
2. Cook noodles in boiling, salted water for 10 minutes. Drain.
3. Melt butter in saucepan, add breadcrumbs, cheese, meat, cooked noodles, milk, salt and pepper and the beaten egg yolks.
4. Mix thoroughly and then fold in the stiffly-beaten egg whites.
5. Pour mixture into a greased soufflé or ovenware dish.
6. Stand dish in a pan of hot water and cook in centre of oven for about 1 hour. Serve with a mixed salad.

NOODLES WITH EGGS AND BACON
Serves 4

12oz (300gm) noodles
6 eggs
salt and pepper
1oz (25gm) butter
8 bacon rashers

1. Cook noodles in boiling, salted water for 10 minutes.
2. Drain. Beat eggs, adding salt and pepper to taste.
3. Melt butter in a saucepan, add noodles and reheat, stirring occasionally.
4. Pour beaten eggs over noodles. Stir until eggs are cooked.
5. Serve on a hot dish with fried bacon rashers.

NOODLES WITH MEAT SAUCE
(Illustrated on page 18)
Serves 4

1 onion, peeled
2oz (50gm) mushrooms, peeled
8oz (200gm) minced meat
1½oz (37gm) butter
½ pint (250ml) stock
salt and pepper
12oz (300gm) noodles
grated Parmesan cheese
3 tablespoons red wine
1 tablespoon chopped parsley
2 tablespoons cream or
natural yogurt
3 tablespoons cooked peas

1. Chop onion and mushrooms finely, mix with meat and fry gently in ½oz (12gm) butter for 5 minutes.
2. Add stock, then season and simmer for 20–30 minutes, until meat is tender.
3. Meanwhile, cook noodles in boiling, salted water for 8–10 minutes, then drain well.
4. Toss in the rest of the butter and some cheese.
5. Add wine, parsley, cream and peas to meat.
6. Cook for 2–3 minutes.
7. Pile noodles on a hot dish and pour sauce over.

TURKEY IN THE STRAW
Serves 4

1 tablespoon salt
8oz (200gm) fine egg noodles
2oz (50gm) butter or margarine
1oz (25gm) plain flour
½ pint (250ml) milk
4oz (100gm) processed cheese,
grated
2 canned pimentos, chopped
8oz (200gm) cooked turkey,
diced
10oz (250gm) fresh, canned or
frozen asparagus, thawed and
diced
salt and pepper

1. Preheat oven to moderate, 350 deg F or gas 4 (180 deg C).
2. Add salt to a large pan of rapidly boiling water.
3. Gradually add noodles and cook uncovered, stirring occasionally, until tender, then drain.
4. Arrange around outer edge of a greased casserole dish and keep hot.
5. Melt butter or margarine in a pan and blend in the flour.
6. Gradually add milk and cook, stirring constantly, until mixture thickens.
7. Add cheese and stir until it has melted.
8. Add remaining ingredients and mix well.
9. Turn into the centre of the casserole dish.
10. Bake for 30 minutes.

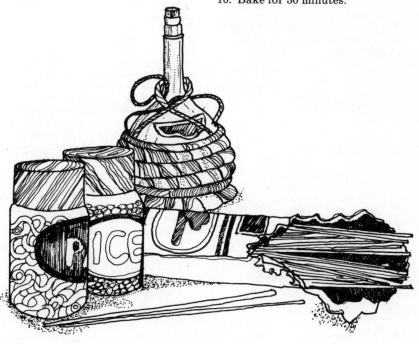

Bacon and ham

Bacon and ham are the basis of some of the most economic and tastiest meals in this book. You'll find lots of family favourites here.

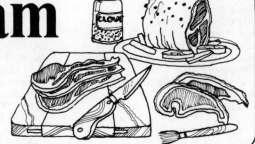

BACON PARCELS
(Illustrated on page 18)
Serves 4

6oz (150gm) bacon rashers
12oz (300gm) chipolata pork sausages
4 whole tomatoes
4oz (100gm) mushrooms, sliced
salt and pepper

1. Preheat oven to moderately hot, 400 deg F or gas 6 (200 deg C).
2. Take the rinds off the bacon and cut rashers in half lengthways.
3. Roll sausages in the pieces of bacon.
4. Arrange in a shallow baking dish with the tomatoes and mushrooms and top with dabs of butter.
5. Sprinkle with salt and pepper and cover tightly with a lid or foil. Bake for 30 minutes on centre shelf of oven.

LIVER AND BACON A LA FRANÇAISE
Serves 4–6

1lb (½ kilo) calf's or sheep's liver
4 tablespoons breadcrumbs
1 small onion, chopped
1 tablespoon chopped parsley
salt and pepper
pinch of nutmeg
1oz (25gm) butter, melted
1 bacon rasher for each slice of liver
½ pint (250ml) stock
1 dessertspoon Worcestershire sauce
a few browned breadcrumbs

1. Preheat oven to moderate, 350 deg F or gas 4 (180 deg C).
2. Slice, wash and dry the liver. Lay slices in a greased ovenware dish.
3. Mix together breadcrumbs, onion, parsley, salt and pepper, nutmeg and butter and put some of this mixture on each piece of liver. Cover with a bacon rasher.
4. Pour the stock and Worcestershire sauce around the liver.
5. Cover with a lid or greased paper and cook in centre of oven for about 40 minutes, until the liver is cooked.
6. Remove the lid, sprinkle a few browned crumbs over the bacon and put back in the oven to crisp.
7. Serve with mashed potatoes and a green vegetable.

BACON AND HERRING ROE TOASTED SANDWICH
Serves 4

4 streaky bacon rashers
2oz (50gm) button mushrooms, sliced
8 large slices bread
butter
1 can (8oz or 200gm) herring roes, drained

1. Remove rind from bacon rashers and grill them until cooked.
2. Snip into ½-inch pieces and combine them with sliced mushrooms.
3. Toast one side of four of the slices of bread, then turn them over.
4. Butter the untoasted side and arrange herring roes on top.
5. Divide the bacon and mushroom mixture between the slices.
6. Return to grill for 3–4 minutes, until filling is hot.
7. Butter one side of each of the remaining slices of bread.
8. Place one on top of each sandwich and return to the grill, until sandwich is browned.
9. Serve hot.

POTATO AND BACON AU GRATIN
Serves 4

1lb (½ kilo) potatoes, boiled
4oz (100gm) streaky bacon, fried and diced
1 can condensed mushroom soup
2 tablespoons milk
3oz (75gm) cheese, grated
1oz (25gm) browned breadcrumbs

1. Preheat oven to hot, 425 deg F or gas 7 (220 deg C).
2. Slice the potatoes and place half in a greased pie dish.
3. Cover with bacon.
4. Mix soup with the milk and pour over the top.
5. Add remainder of potatoes and cover with a mixture of cheese and breadcrumbs.
6. Cook on centre shelf of oven for 15 minutes, until heated through.

BACON AND EGG HASH
Serves 4

2 small onions
1oz (25gm) butter
8oz (200gm) streaky bacon rashers
1lb (½ kilo) potatoes
1 pint (approximately ½ litre) stock
3 eggs

1. Skin the onions and chop finely.
2. Heat the butter and cook the onions until tender.
3. Remove rind from bacon. Chop into small pieces and add to the onion.
4. Peel, slice and add the potatoes to the onion mixture.
5. Add the stock, reduce heat and cook for 30 minutes.
6. Add a little more stock if required, to prevent sticking.
7. Poach the eggs.
8. Serve bacon mixture in a hot dish topped with the eggs.

CRISPY VEGETABLE AND BACON CASSEROLE
Serves 4

8oz (200gm) onions or leeks, sliced
8oz (200gm) carrots, sliced
4oz (100gm) mushrooms, sliced
6oz (150gm) lean bacon rashers
1 small can creamed corn
1 small can peas
pinch of marjoram
salt and pepper
3–4 tablespoons water
½oz (12gm) flour
crushed potato crisps
grated cheese

1. Preheat oven to moderate, 350 deg F or gas 4 (180 deg C).
2. Butter a casserole or pie dish.
3. Prepare onions, carrots and mushrooms. De-rind bacon and cut rashers into small pieces.
4. Arrange in layers in the casserole or pie dish with creamed corn, peas, marjoram and seasoning.
5. Pour water over and cover with a lid.
6. Cook in centre of oven for 1½–2 hours, or until tender.
7. Drain off liquid and thicken it with the flour.
8. Pour it back over the ingredients in the casserole. Top with a mixture of crushed crisps and grated cheese.

BACON AND FISH CURLS
Serves 4

8 back bacon rashers
8 small plaice fillets
salt and pepper
lemon juice
sprigs of parsley to garnish

1. Preheat oven to moderate, 350 deg F or gas 4 (180 deg C).
2. Cut off the bacon rinds and flatten the rashers with the back of a knife on a board.
3. Lay a plaice fillet on each rasher.
4. Sprinkle with salt and pepper and a squeeze of lemon juice.
5. Roll up the rashers and bake for about 25 minutes.
6. Garnish with parsley sprigs.

BOILED BACON WITH STUFFED ONIONS
Serves 4

2½lb (approximately 1¼ kilo) piece of collar bacon
4 medium onions
2oz (50gm) mushrooms
1 teaspoon tomato purée
salt and pepper
1oz (25gm) butter
tomato sauce

1. Preheat oven to moderate, 350 deg F or gas 4 (180 deg C).
2. Place bacon in a pan and cover with water.
3. Bring to the boil and pour away the water, replacing it with fresh.
4. Bring to the boil again and simmer for 20 minutes to the pound (½ kilo) and 20 minutes over.
5. Skin the onions and boil them for 10 minutes.
6. Cut them in half horizontally and slice the ends so that they stand firmly.
7. Scoop out part of the centre flesh and chop it with the mushrooms.
8. Mix together with the tomato purée, salt and pepper.
9. Return the mixture to the onion shells and dot the top of each with a little butter.
10. Bake the stuffed onions for about 20 minutes, until tender.
11. Serve with a little tomato sauce on each.
12. De-rind the bacon and place it in a dish with the onions. Serve with creamed potatoes and additional vegetables.

BACON PIE
Serves 6

3 tablespoons olive oil
2 large onions, skinned and sliced
1 green pepper
1 red pepper
12oz (300gm) piece of collar bacon, cooked and cut in cubes
4 tomatoes, skinned and sliced
1 can whole kernel sweetcorn, drained
1 small packet frozen peas
salt and pepper
dash of Worcestershire sauce
½oz (12gm) flour
1 pint (approximately ½ litre) stock
2 tablespoons tomato purée
shortcrust pastry made with 8oz (200gm) flour (see Basic recipes, page 100)

1. Preheat oven to moderate, 350 deg F or gas 4 (180 deg C).
2. Heat the oil in a pan and fry onions until tender but not browned. Keep hot on a plate.
3. Seed peppers and slice very thinly. Sauté for 2 minutes in the oil.
4. Add to the onions and turn into a large pie dish or casserole.
5. Stir in bacon cubes, tomatoes, half the corn and half the peas.
6. Season and add Worcestershire sauce.
7. Reheat the oil and stir in the flour.
8. Remove from heat and blend in stock and tomato purée. Pour this over bacon. Top with remaining corn and peas.
9. Bake in centre of oven for 45 minutes. Allow to cool.
10. Cover with pastry and bake in a moderately hot oven, 400 deg F or gas 6 (200 deg C) for a further 30 minutes.
11. Serve at once, very hot.

BACON AND SAUSAGE SLICES
Serves 4

1 onion
¼ pint (125ml) milk
4 medium thick slices short back bacon
2 teaspoons prepared mustard
8oz (200gm) sausagemeat
1 egg yolk
2oz (50gm) stale breadcrumbs
bacon dripping or lard for frying
a little flour
3 tomatoes

1. Skin and slice the onion. Put it to soak in a little milk.
2. Spread bacon slices sparingly with mustard.
3. Divide sausagemeat into four portions.
4. With floured hands, mould the sausagemeat round the rashers of bacon, then flatten them neatly with a lightly floured rolling pin.
5. Mix egg yolk with a teaspoon of cold water and brush over the slices.
6. Coat slices with breadcrumbs. Fry in the bacon dripping or lard, on both sides, until golden brown.
7. Drain on kitchen paper and keep hot.
8. Drain onion rings well and dust them with flour.
9. Fry them in the fat left over after frying the bacon slices, adding a little more if necessary.
10. Slice the tomatoes thickly and fry lightly.
11. Arrange tomatoes and bacon slices on a hot serving dish. Garnish with onion rings.
12. Serve hot with creamed potatoes and vegetables.

BACON PASTIES
Serves 4

shortcrust pastry made with 8oz (200gm) flour (see Basic recipes, page 100)
8oz (200gm) cold, cooked bacon
1 small potato, cooked
1 onion, finely chopped
4 tablespoons stock
1 tablespoon chopped parsley

1. Preheat oven to moderately hot, 400 deg F or gas 6 (200 deg C).
2. Divide the shortcrust pastry into four pieces and roll each into a round the size of a saucer.
3. Dice bacon and potato and mix with the onion, stock and parsley.
4. Moisten the edges of the pastry rounds and place a quarter of the filling in the middle of each one.
5. Join the edges of the pastry over the top and crimp together, making sure they stick.
6. Put on to a baking tin and bake for 20 minutes, then reduce the heat to very moderate, 325 deg F, or gas 3 (170 deg C) for a further 20 minutes. (If they are browning too much, cover them with foil.)
7. Serve hot or cold.

BACON AND APPLE ROLL
Serves 4–6

shortcrust pastry made with 8oz (200gm) flour (see Basic recipes, page 100)
1lb (½ kilo) cooked bacon, minced
1 large cooking apple, chopped
sage to taste
1 egg, beaten

1. Preheat oven to hot, 425 deg F or gas 7 (220 deg C).
2. Roll out the pastry into a rectangle.
3. Mix the bacon, apple and sage.
4. Spread this mixture on the pastry.
5. Moisten edges with water and roll up, starting from a long side.
6. Brush with egg, slash top and decorate with pastry leaves.
7. Bake in centre of oven for 10–15 minutes.
8. Reduce heat to moderate, 350 deg F or gas 4 (180 deg C), and cook for a further 20 minutes.
9. Serve hot or cold.

SCOTCH EGGS MADE WITH BACON
Serves 4–6

2 small onions, chopped
1oz (25gm) butter
1 tablespoon plain flour
12oz (300gm) cooked bacon,
minced
3 tablespoons brown
breadcrumbs
herbs to taste
pepper
6 hard-boiled eggs
1 egg, beaten
breadcrumbs for coating
deep fat for frying

1. Fry onions in a little butter.
2. Meanwhile add flour to the
bacon.
3. Add to this the breadcrumbs,
herbs and onion, and season with
pepper.
4. Divide mixture into six.
5. Shell the eggs and mould a
portion of bacon mixture around
each.
6. Brush each with beaten egg
and coat with breadcrumbs.
7. Leave to 'set' for 30 minutes,
then fry in hot deep fat until
golden brown. Drain and serve
hot or cold.

BACON FRITTERS
Serves 4

1½oz (37gm) plain flour
salt and pepper
1 dessertspoon chopped onion
1 egg
milk
4oz (100gm) lean bacon,
chopped
1 teaspoon baking powder
deep fat for frying

1. Mix the flour, seasoning and
onion.
2. Add the egg and gradually stir
in milk to make a stiff batter.
Beat well.
3. Add the bacon and baking
powder to the batter.
4. Drop teaspoonfuls of mixture
into deep, hot fat, and fry until
golden brown.
5. Drain and serve very hot.

SUGARED HAM
(Illustrated on page 18)
Serves 4

1 can (2lb or 1 kilo) ham
1oz (25gm) demerara sugar
½oz (12gm) cloves
1 can peach halves
1 small can prunes
1 lettuce

1. Preheat oven to hot, 450 deg F
or gas 8 (230 deg C).
2. Remove ham from the can and
sprinkle thickly with demarara
sugar.
3. Stud with cloves and put in a
small roasting tin.
4. Bake in centre of oven for
approximately 10 minutes, until
sugar turns golden brown.
5. Turn oven temperature down
to very cool, 250 deg F, or gas ½
(130 deg C), and leave ham in oven
for a further 20 minutes.
6. Drain peaches and prunes, then
stone prunes.
7. Place ham on a bed of lettuce
on a serving dish and surround
with peach halves and prunes.

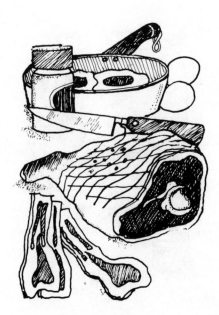

HAM AND BEAN CASSEROLE
Serves 4

6oz (150gm) haricot beans,
soaked overnight
1lb (½ kilo) ham or bacon
2 sticks celery, sliced
1 large onion, sliced
1 tablespoon sugar
1 tablespoon treacle
½ teaspoon mustard
salt and pepper

1. Preheat oven to very moderate,
325 deg F or gas 3 (170 deg C).
2. Drain the beans.
3. Cut the ham in large pieces and
put in a casserole dish.
4. Add the beans.
5. Add the other ingredients and
enough water to just cover.
6. Cover the dish and bake for
about 4 hours, adding water from
time to time, if necessary.

DEVILLED HAM
Serves 4

1½oz (37gm) butter
½ teaspoon cayenne pepper
1 teaspoon ground ginger
pinch of black pepper
½ teaspoon curry powder
1 teaspoon piquant sauce
4 slices ham
parsley to garnish

1. Pound or blend butter,
cayenne, ginger, pepper, curry
powder and piquant sauce
together.
2. Spread the ham fairly
generously with the mixture.
3. Put under a hot grill and cook
until brown. Garnish with parsley.

PINEAPPLE AND HAM WITH TARRAGON CREAM DRESSING
Serves 6

2 small pineapples
juice of 1 lemon
2½oz (62gm) caster sugar
1 egg
3 tablespoons tarragon vinegar
salt and pepper
3 tablespoons cream, lightly whipped
paprika pepper
8 slices ham

1. Cut the pineapples in two lengthways, scoop out core and dice all the flesh very finely.
2. Sprinkle with lemon juice and dust with ½oz (12gm) caster sugar. Leave to stand in a cold place.
3. Beat the egg in a basin, add the rest of the sugar, and vinegar.
4. Cook over a pan of hot water until mixture thickens and has a creamy consistency.
5. Leave to cool and season lightly. Fold in the cream.
6. Return the diced pineapple to the pineapple shells and pour the dressing over.
7. Sprinkle with paprika pepper.
8. Serve very cold with the slices of ham rolled on top of each pineapple half.

HAM MADEIRA
Serves 4

1oz (25gm) butter
2 tablespoons powdered tomato soup
½ teaspoon paprika pepper
pinch of ground nutmeg
½ pint (250ml) water
1 glass Madeira or sherry
8oz (200gm) cooked ham, sliced

1. Melt butter and mix to a paste with soup powder, paprika pepper and nutmeg.
2. Add water gradually and bring to boil, stirring well.
3. Boil for 5 minutes, then add Madeira or sherry and cook for a further 5 minutes.
4. Place the ham in a hot serving dish and pour the sauce over.

HAM ON TOAST
Serves 4

8oz (200gm) cottage cheese
4oz (100gm) ham, cut into narrow strips
1 teaspoon prepared mustard
salt and pepper
8 slices bread
2oz (50gm) butter for spreading

1. Mix together cottage cheese, ham, mustard, salt and pepper.
2. Cut crusts off the bread and toast it.
3. Butter each slice and top four of them with cottage cheese mixture.
4. Grill for 2 minutes, then top each with a piece of toast, to make four sandwiches.

MINCED HAM WITH POACHED EGGS
Serves 4

6oz (150gm) cooked ham, minced or chopped
¼ pint (125ml) white sauce (see Basic recipes, page 100)
¼ teaspoon mustard
a little tomato ketchup
4 rounds buttered toast
4 poached eggs

1. Mix the ham with the sauce, mustard and ketchup.
2. Spoon on to hot toast and serve with the poached eggs on top.
3. Serve extra toast, if desired.

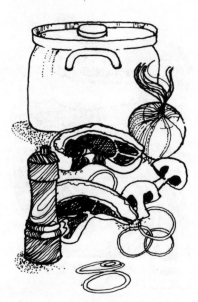

CRISPY WELSH BAKE
Serves 4

1 packet sage and onion stuffing
4oz (100gm) cheese, grated
4 leeks, washed and trimmed
4 slices cooked ham
1 can cream of mushroom soup

1. Preheat oven to moderate to moderately hot, 375 deg F or gas 5 (190 deg C).
2. Mix together stuffing and cheese.
3. Cook leeks in boiling, salted water until tender, then drain.
4. Roll each leek in a slice of ham. Place in an ovenware dish.
5. Pour the soup over and sprinkle with the stuffing and cheese mixture.
6. Bake for about 30 minutes until the topping is golden.
7. Serve hot.

HAM AND EGG LUNCH DISH
Serves 4

4 hard-boiled eggs
8oz (200gm) cooked ham
salt and pepper
4oz (100gm) butter
6 tablespoons brown crumbs
½ pint (250ml) white sauce (see Basic recipes, page 100)
toast triangles

1. Preheat oven to moderate, 350 deg F or gas 4 (180 deg C).
2. Roughly chop up the eggs and ham and season lightly.
3. Melt the fat and mix with the crumbs. Put a layer of this into a pie dish, then a layer of egg mixed with ham, followed by some white sauce.
4. Continue, finishing with a layer of crumbs.
5. Bake in the oven for 30 minutes.
6. Garnish with triangles of toast.

HAM WITH SPICY RICE SALAD
Serves 4

1lb (½ kilo) ham
2oz (50gm) butter
3oz (75gm) boiled long-grain rice (raw weight)
salt and prepared mustard
1 garlic clove, crushed
2–3 tablespoons French dressing (see Basic recipes, page 100)
1 tablespoon tomato ketchup

1. Slice ham downwards, into eight slices and fry in butter.
2. Mix the rice with salt and mustard to taste.
3. Add garlic and French dressing and stir in the tomato ketchup.
4. Serve with the hot fried ham.

EGG AND HAM CHARLOTTE
Serves 4

2oz (50gm) lean, cooked ham
3 hard-boiled eggs
1½oz (37gm) butter
2oz (50gm) mushrooms, chopped
2 sticks celery, chopped
1½oz (37gm) flour
¾ pint (375ml) milk
salt and pepper
3–4 tablespoons fresh breadcrumbs
butter

1. Preheat oven to moderate, 350 deg F or gas 4 (180 deg C).
2. Chop the ham and place it in an ovenware dish.
3. Slice the eggs and add them to the ham.
4. Melt 1oz (25gm) of the butter and fry the mushrooms and celery for 10 minutes.
5. Mix in the flour with a wooden spoon, then remove the pan from the heat.
6. Add the milk gradually, stirring all the time.
7. Return it to the heat, bring to the boil and season to taste.
8. Pour this sauce over the eggs. Cover with breadcrumbs and dot with remaining butter.
9. Bake for 15–20 minutes, until breadcrumbs are crisp and golden.

HAM AND MUSHROOM PIZZAS
Serves 4

¼ pint (125ml) milk
1 teaspoon lemon juice
8oz (200gm) self-raising flour
pinch of salt
2oz (50gm) butter
12oz (300gm) Lancashire cheese, crumbled
4 large tomatoes, skinned and sliced
salt and pepper
pinch of mixed herbs
2oz (50gm) ham, cut into strips
2oz (50gm) mushrooms, sliced and fried

1. Preheat oven to hot, 450 deg F or gas 8 (230 deg C).
2. Mix milk and lemon juice together and leave to stand for 5 minutes.
3. Sift flour and salt into a bowl, then rub butter in.
4. Mix to a soft dough with milk and lemon juice.
5. Turn dough on to a floured board and knead lightly until smooth.
6. Divide into four and shape dough into flat rounds about a ¼ inch thick.
7. Place rounds on a large greased baking tray and cover with alternate layers of cheese and tomato. Reserve a few tomato slices.
8. Sprinkle salt, pepper and mixed herbs between each layer.
9. Top with ham, mushrooms, and remaining tomato slices.
10. Bake near top of oven until well risen.
11. Serve immediately.

HAM AND BEAN TART
Serves 4–6

shortcrust pastry made with 8oz (200gm) flour (see Basic recipes, page 100)
12oz (300gm) ham, minced
2 hard-boiled eggs, chopped
1 medium can baked beans in tomato sauce
salt and pepper
little milk

1. Preheat oven to moderate to moderately hot, 375 deg F or gas 5 (190 deg C).
2. Roll out pastry and use half of it to line an 8-inch (20cm) flan case.
3. Mix together ham, eggs, baked beans and seasoning. Place in the flan case.
4. Roll out remainder of pastry to make a top for the tart.
5. Cover and seal the edges well and decorate with pastry leaves. Brush with a little milk.
6. Bake in oven for 30–35 minutes until pastry is golden.
7. Serve hot or cold.

HAM AND CHICKEN PASTIES
Makes 4

8oz (200gm) potatoes, cooked and diced
1 can ham and chicken roll, cut into ½-inch cubes
1 tomato, skinned and roughly chopped
good pinch of mixed herbs
salt and pepper
shortcrust pastry made with 8oz (200gm) flour (see Basic recipes, page 100)
beaten egg or milk to glaze

1. Preheat oven to moderately hot, 400 deg F or gas 6 (200 deg C).
2. Mix together potatoes, meat, tomato, herbs and seasoning.
3. Divide the pastry into four pieces. Roll out each piece to a circle about 8 inches in diameter and brush the edges with water.
4. Put a quarter of the filling into each circle. Fold in half and seal the edges.
5. Brush with beaten egg or milk and bake in centre of oven for 10 minutes.
6. Reduce the oven setting to moderate, 350 deg F or gas 4 (180 deg C) for a further 10 minutes.
7. Serve hot or cold.

GAMMON IN CIDER
Serves 4

4 gammon steaks
2 level teaspoons mustard
2 level tablespoons brown sugar
½ pint (250ml) cider
2 level teaspoons cornflour
2 tablespoons cream or top of the milk
1 teaspoon chopped parsley

1. Preheat oven to moderately hot, 400 deg F or gas 6 (200 deg C).
2. Put the gammon into a small casserole.
3. Mix the mustard with the sugar and 1 tablespoon of cider. Spread this over the gammon steaks.
4. Leave for 15 minutes.
5. Pour the rest of the cider over the gammon and cover with a lid.
6. Put into centre of oven for 20 minutes.
7. Drain off the liquid into a saucepan and keep the gammon hot.
8. Blend the cornflour with just enough cold water to make a cream and stir it into the hot liquid.
9. Stir the sauce over a gentle heat until it boils.
10. Add the cream or top of the milk, off the heat.
11. Pour the sauce over the gammon and sprinkle with parsley.

HAM IN ASPIC
Serves 4

8 slices ham
1 pint (approximately ½ litre) liquid aspic jelly (see Basic recipes, page 100)
4oz (100gm) button mushrooms
8 gherkins
3 tomatoes

1. Arrange slices of ham on a serving dish.
2. Pour over just enough aspic jelly to cover. Arrange sliced mushrooms, gherkins and tomatoes round the edge of the plate.
3. Pour the remaining aspic over and leave to set in a cold place.

GAMMON AND ORANGE
(Illustrated on page 35)
Serves 4

4 slices gammon
2 tablespoons marmalade
1oz (25gm) brown sugar
2 oranges

1. Preheat the grill. Trim the rind from the gammon and snip the fat; brush one side of each piece with some marmalade.
2. Sprinkle with some brown sugar and grill for 5 minutes.
3. Turn the slices, put rest of marmalade and sugar on the second side.
4. Grill for a further 5–6 minutes, until the gammon is cooked.
5. Peel and slice the oranges and serve with the gammon.

GAMMON WITH PINEAPPLE AND CIDER SAUCE
Serves 4

1 level tablespoon cornflour
½ pint (250ml) dry cider
4oz (100gm) fresh or canned pineapple, chopped
1oz (25gm) seedless raisins
4 gammon slices

1. Blend cornflour with 2 tablespoons cider.
2. Heat remaining cider in a saucepan.
3. Stir on to blended cornflour.
4. Return to heat, bring to the boil, stirring well.
5. Add pineapple and raisins and heat through.
6. Grill the gammon slices and pour the sauce over them.

BAKED GAMMON SLICES
Serves 4

4 gammon slices
1 orange
3 level tablespoons bottled cranberry-orange relish
1 level tablespoon brown sugar
½ small onion, finely chopped
1 level tablespoon cornflour
1 tablespoon water

1. Preheat oven to moderate, 350 deg F or gas 4 (180 deg C).
2. Remove rind from gammon and place in a baking tin.
3. Grate the rind of the orange. Segment the flesh and mix any juice with the cranberry-orange relish.
4. Mix together the brown sugar, onion, cranberry-orange relish and orange rind.
5. Pour over the gammon and allow to marinate for 45 minutes, turning once.
6. Cover with cooking foil and bake in centre of oven for 50–60 minutes until tender.
7. Arrange the orange segments on top of the gammon 15 minutes before the end of the cooking time.
8. Strain the liquor into a saucepan and keep the steaks hot.
9. Blend the cornflour with the water and stir into the liquor.
10. Bring to the boil, simmer for 1 minute, pour over the gammon and serve at once.

HONEY-SPICED GAMMON
Serves 4

6 gammon rashers
1oz (25gm) cloves
5 tablespoons clear honey
1 teaspoon brown sugar
¼ teaspoon allspice
salt and pepper
1 teaspoon prepared mustard

1. Slash the gammon rashers round the edges and stud edges with cloves.
2. Put honey, sugar, allspice and seasoning in a saucepan and heat gently.
3. Mix in mustard.
4. Brush this glaze over the gammon rashers.
5. Grill on both sides, brushing several more times with the glaze.

SAUCED GAMMON RASHERS
Serves 4

4 gammon rashers
2oz (50gm) lard
3 tablespoons vinegar
3 tablespoons redcurrant jelly
2 teaspoons prepared mustard
1 teaspoon paprika pepper
1oz (25gm) brown sugar

1. Trim the gammon and snip round the edges.
2. Fry on both sides in the lard. Remove and keep hot.
3. Add vinegar, redcurrant jelly, mustard, sugar and paprika pepper to the pan. Cook slowly for 2 minutes.
4. Serve the gammon on a hot dish topped with the sauce.
5. Accompany with green peas and fried tomato halves.

CHEESE AND GAMMON CASSEROLE
Serves 4

3oz (75gm) butter
2oz (50gm) plain flour
½ pint (250ml) rich stock
3oz (75gm) cheese, grated
salt and pepper
2 onions, finely chopped
6 mushrooms, sliced
6oz (150gm) pork sausage meat, sliced
6 slices cooked gammon

1. Preheat oven to moderate, 350 deg F or gas 4 (180 deg C).
2. Melt 1½oz (37gm) butter in a pan, add the flour and cook over the heat for a few moments.
3. Remove and gradually beat in the stock.
4. Cook until mixture thickens and then stir in the cheese. Season and keep hot.
5. Put the rest of the butter in a frying pan.
6. Add onions, mushrooms and sausage meat and cook gently for 5 minutes.
7. Mix into the sauce.
8. Spoon a little on to each slice of gammon and fold in half.
9. Cover and bake in centre of oven for 15 minutes.

CHEESE AND GAMMON PIE
Serves 4

shortcrust pastry made with 8oz (200gm) flour (see Basic recipes, page 100)
2 large tomatoes
2 hard-boiled eggs
8oz (200gm) gammon
1½oz (37gm) soft cooking fat
1oz (25gm) flour
½ pint (250ml) milk
4oz (100gm) cheese, grated
½ teaspoon mustard
salt and pepper

1. Preheat oven to moderately hot, 400 deg F or gas 6 (200 deg C).
2. Roll out half the pastry and line a ¾-pint (375ml) pie dish.
3. Slice the tomatoes and eggs.
4. Cut gammon into 1-inch pieces.
5. Heat ½oz (12gm) fat in a frying pan and fry gammon. Remove from pan and drain.
6. Melt rest of fat in a saucepan. Stir in the flour, remove from heat and beat in the milk.
7. Bring to the boil, stirring continuously, and cook for 1–2 minutes.
8. Mix in the cheese, mustard and seasoning. Add the cooked gammon.
9. Pour half this sauce into the pastry case. Cover with the sliced eggs and then add the rest of the sauce.
10. Top with sliced tomatoes and allow to cool.
11. Roll out remaining pastry and cover the pie. Trim and decorate the edge. Make two holes in the centre of the pie to allow the steam to escape.
12. Bake in centre of oven for about 40 minutes, or until the pastry is golden brown.

HAM BAKE
Serves 4–6

3¼lb (approximately 1¾ kilo) smoked or green bacon (corner piece is best)
1 pint (approximately ½ litre) cider
1 pint (approximately ½ litre) stock
3 tablespoons clear honey
1 level tablespoon dry mustard
12 cloves

1. Preheat oven to moderate, 350 deg F or gas 4 (180 deg C).
2. Soak the ham overnight.
3. Place in a saucepan and cover with enough cider and stock to cover the joint.
4. Bring to the boil and reduce the heat to simmer for 1¼ hours.
5. Meanwhile, blend the honey and mustard together.
6. Remove the ham from the pan. Skin it and spread the mustard and honey mixture over the skin.
7. Score into diamond shapes and press a whole clove into each diamond.
8. Transfer the joint to a roasting tin and bake in oven for 35 minutes.
9. Serve hot or cold.

SWEET NUTTY GAMMON
Serves 4–6

Roast gammon with a honey and nut crust.

2lb (1 kilo) gammon
6oz (150gm) dripping
1 level teaspoon mixed spice
2oz (50gm) honey
2oz (50gm) nuts, chopped
parsley to garnish

1. Preheat oven to moderately hot, 400 deg F or gas 6 (200 deg C).
2. Wrap gammon with the dripping in kitchen foil. Bake in oven for 45 minutes.
3. Remove foil, skin and score fat. Sprinkle with spice, and baste.
4. Cook for a further 10 minutes.
5. Pour off basting fat. Mix the honey and nuts and spread over the joint.
6. Return to the oven to brown.
7. Garnish with parsley.

Fish

Fish has the advantage of being both nutritious and quick to cook. It is still relatively economic and can be stretched to go a bit further with a tasty sauce.

VALENCIA PANCAKES
Serves 4

2lb (1 kilo) fresh cod
2 lemons
1oz (25gm) butter
1oz (25gm) flour
1 pint (approximately ½ litre) milk
4oz (100gm) mushrooms
1 tablespoon sweet sherry
salt and pepper
½ pint (250ml) pancake batter (see Basic recipes, page 100)
2oz (50gm) cheese, grated
2–4oz (50–100gm) flaked almonds

1. Boil cod in salted water to which juice of 2 lemons has been added. Simmer for 20–25 minutes.
2. Skin the fish, remove bones and flake.
3. Melt butter in a pan and stir in flour. Cook for 2 minutes, then gradually stir in the milk, beating steadily.
4. Add finely chopped mushrooms and the sherry. Simmer for 5 minutes and season to taste.
5. Mix flaked fish into half the sauce.
6. Make 6 pancakes with batter and coat each one with 2 tablespoons fish mixture. Roll each pancake up and place in a shallow, ovenware dish.
7. Cover with remaining sauce, sprinkle with cheese and flaked almonds and brown under the grill just before serving.

COD WITH GRAPES
(Illustrated on page 36)
Serves 4

4 cod cutlets
1 shallot, sliced
2oz (50gm) button mushrooms, sliced
1 pint (approximately ½ litre) fish stock
a little white wine (optional)
salt and pepper
1oz (25gm) butter
1oz (25gm) flour
¼ pint (125ml) milk
4oz (100gm) white grapes, skinned and seeded
watercress to garnish

1. Preheat oven to moderate to moderately hot, 375 deg F or gas 5 (190 deg C).
2. Wash the fish and put into a baking dish.
3. Add the shallot and mushrooms. Cover with stock and the wine, if used.
4. Season, and bake on centre shelf of oven for 20 minutes.
5. Reserve ¼ pint (125ml) of the liquid. Discard onion; reserve mushrooms and keep hot.
6. Arrange the fish on a dish.
7. To make a sauce, melt the butter in a saucepan and add the flour.
8. Remove from heat and gradually stir in stock and the milk.
9. Season and boil sauce, stirring, until it thickens. Add most of the grapes.
10. Pour sauce over the fish and garnish with watercress, the rest of the grapes and mushrooms.

FISH PIE DE LUXE
Serves 4

1lb (½ kilo) cod or haddock
½ pint (250ml) milk
2oz (50gm) butter
1 small onion, skinned
salt and pepper
1 level tablespoon cornflour
2 hard-boiled eggs
2oz (50gm) prawns
1½lb (¾ kilo) hot, mashed potato
parsley
lemon slices

1. Preheat oven to moderately hot, 400 deg F or gas 6 (200 deg C).
2. Put the fish in a pan with the milk, butter, quartered onion and seasoning.
3. Simmer for 10 minutes, then lift the fish into a pie dish, removing bones and skin.
4. Strain the remaining liquid, making it up to ½ pint (250ml) if necessary, with milk. Discard the onion.
5. Blend the cornflour with 1 tablespoon water and stir into the liquid in the pan.
6. Simmer for 3 minutes, stirring well.
7. Slice the eggs into the pie dish.
8. Add the prawns, keeping a few for garnish.
9. Pour the sauce over and top with a layer of potato.
10. Place in centre of oven for 20–30 minutes, until brown on top.
11. Garnish with the remaining prawns, the parsley and lemon slices.

STUFFED COD CUTLETS
Serves 4

1½lb (¾ kilo) cod, cut into 4
cutlets
½ pint (250ml) shelled shrimps
4oz (100gm) fresh breadcrumbs
salt and pepper
2 teaspoons lemon juice
2 eggs, beaten
flour
breadcrumbs

1. Preheat oven to moderate to
moderately hot, 375 deg F or gas 5
(190 deg C).
2. Dry the cutlets thoroughly.
3. Mix together the shrimps,
breadcrumbs, seasoning and
lemon juice. Bind together with
a little of the egg.
4. Spread the mixture on one side
of the cutlets only, coat each
cutlet in flour, then in egg and
breadcrumbs.
5. Arrange in an ovenware dish,
cover and bake for 40 minutes.

FISH CURRY
(Illustrated on page 36)
Serves 4

1 large onion, chopped
2oz (50gm) butter
3 tomatoes, skinned and
quartered
1½lb (¾ kilo) cod fillet
2 teaspoons curry powder
salt
pinch of sugar

1. Fry onion in butter and add the
tomatoes.
2. Skin fish, cut into pieces and
coat with curry powder.
3. Fry fish until brown, then add
salt and sugar.
4. Cover and simmer for 10
minutes.
5. Serve with hot rice and
poppadoms.

CRUNCHY FISH BAKE
Serves 4

1 packet (13oz or 325gm) cod
fillets or steaks
1 can condensed mushroom
soup
4oz (100gm) Cheddar cheese,
grated
2oz (50gm) browned
breadcrumbs
1 small packet potato crisps,
crushed

1. Preheat oven to moderate to
moderately hot, 375 deg F or gas 5
(190 deg C).
2. Place pieces of fish in an
ovenproof dish. Pour soup over.
3. Mix cheese, breadcrumbs and
crisps together and sprinkle over
soup.
4. Bake in oven for 20–25 minutes.

FRIDAY CURRY
Serves 4

8oz (200gm) long-grain rice
1 onion, chopped
½ apple, chopped
2 sticks celery, chopped
2oz (50gm) margarine
1 packet (12oz or 300gm) frozen
cod fillets, cut into portions
and seasoned with salt and
pepper
1 can curry sauce
3 tablespoons water
1 tablespoon lemon juice
1 tablespoon chopped parsley
lemon slices

1. Cook rice for 15 minutes in
boiling, salted water until tender.
2. Fry the onion, apple and celery
in the margarine until tender.
3. Add the fish portions and cook
for 10 minutes.
4. Add the curry sauce and water
and simmer for 5 minutes.
5. Drain the rice and place
around the edge of a hot serving
dish.
6. Lift the fish out of the sauce
and place in the centre of the rice.
7. Add the lemon juice to the
sauce and pour over the fish.
8. Garnish the fish with parsley
and put the lemon slices on the
rice.

CURRIED COD BOMBAY
Serves 4

1½lb (¾ kilo) cod fillet
2 dessertspoons curry powder
1 dessertspoon flour
1 dessertspoon cornflour
4oz (100gm) butter
1lb (½ kilo) mushrooms
1 tablespoon chopped onion
salt and pepper
1 egg
½ pint (250ml) fish stock

1. Cut the fish into 3-inch pieces.
2. Mix 1 teaspoon curry powder
with the flour and cornflour and
coat the fish thoroughly with this
mixture.
3. Cook the fish in 1oz (25gm)
butter until just tender. Put to
one side.
4. Finely chop the mushrooms
and fry them with the onion and
2oz (50gm) butter.
5. Add salt and pepper and
simmer very gently until the
onion is tender.
6. Beat in the egg and return to
heat for a minute.
7. Set the mushroom mixture on
a hot dish and top with the fish
pieces.
8. Heat the remaining butter and
stir in the fish stock with rest of
curry powder.
9. Bring to the boil and simmer
for 5 minutes.
10. Check the seasoning and pour
over the fish.

CRUSTY-TOPPED COD
Serves 4

2oz (50gm) petite Gruyère
salt and pepper
1 level teaspoon mixed herbs
1 egg, beaten
4 cod cutlets, about 4oz (100gm)
each
juice of ½ lemon
½oz (12gm) butter or margarine

1. Sieve the petite Gruyère
cheese, add salt, pepper, mixed
herbs and bind with egg.
2. Wash the cutlets and brush
with lemon juice.
3. Place a knob of butter or
margarine on each side.
4. Grill for 6 minutes on one side.
Turn and grill for 3 minutes on
other side.
5. Spread with the cheese
topping and grill for a further 3
minutes.
6. Serve hot, with grilled
tomatoes and creamed potatoes.

CRISPY FISH PIE
Serves 6

cheese pastry made with 6oz
(150gm) flour (see Basic
recipes, page 100)
1 small can evaporated milk
2 eggs, lightly beaten
1 large packet frozen cod
fillets, diced
1 onion, finely chopped
2 sticks celery, chopped
2 teaspoons prepared mustard
1 tablespoon capers
½ level teaspoon ground ginger
salt and pepper
3–4 small potatoes
2 tablespoons oil

1. Preheat oven to moderate, 350
deg F or gas 4 (180 deg C).
2. Roll out pastry and line a deep,
9-inch (23cm) pie plate.
3. Mix together the evaporated
milk, eggs, fish, onion, celery,
mustard, capers, ginger and
seasoning. Pour into the pastry
case.
4. Arrange, overlapping, thin
slices of potato to cover the
surface. Brush with oil.
5. Bake on centre shelf of oven
for 45 minutes.
6. Serve hot.

ITALIAN FISH
Serves 4

4 cod cutlets or hake fillets
2oz (50gm) butter
1 garlic clove, finely chopped
1 teaspoon chopped chives
6 mushrooms
1 tablespoon chopped parsley
1 teaspoon flour
2–3 tablespoons stock
¼ pint (125ml) white wine
salt and pepper
olive oil
parsley to garnish

1. Prepare the fish.
2. Melt the butter in a saucepan,
add the garlic, chives, sliced
mushrooms and parsley. Cook for
a few minutes.
3. Stir in the flour and cook for a
further 3 minutes.
4. Add the stock and wine
gradually, stirring; season. Bring
to the boil, then cover and simmer
gently for 10 minutes.
5. Meanwhile, fry the fillets in
oil. Drain and put into a hot dish.
6. Cover with the sauce and
garnish with parsley.

FISH PANCAKES
Serves 4

½ pint (250ml) pancake batter
(see Basic recipes, page 100)
1oz (25gm) lard
½ onion, chopped
1oz (25gm) butter
1oz (25gm) flour
½ pint (250ml) stock
6oz (150gm) cod, cooked and
flaked
1 hard-boiled egg, chopped
2 teaspoons chopped parsley
salt and pepper
1 tablespoon cream

1. Pour a little batter into a small
frying pan, lightly greased with
lard. Cook each pancake until
brown on both sides and keep
them hot.
2. Cook onion in butter until
tender, and sprinkle with flour.
3. Stir and cook over a low heat
for 1 minute.
4. Add the stock and, stirring,
bring to the boil.
5. Add fish, egg, parsley, seasoning and cream.
6. Reheat and fill pancakes with
this mixture. Serve hot.

COD SOUFFLE LEONI
Serves 4

8oz (200gm) cooked cod fillet
1oz (25gm) onion, chopped
1oz (25gm) lard
1 dessertspoon tomato purée
1½oz (37gm) flour
⅓ pint (170ml) boiling water
salt and pepper
4oz (100gm) mushrooms
1 small glass sherry
1 teaspoon chopped parsley
2–3oz (50–75gm) prawns or
shrimps
1½oz (37gm) cheese, grated
2oz (50gm) butter
½ pint (250ml) milk
4 eggs
paprika
4oz (100gm) long grain rice
lemon slices

1. Preheat oven to hot, 425 deg F
or gas 7 (220 deg C).
2. Flake the fish finely.
3. Toss onion in lard until soft
but not brown. Add tomato purée,
stir well and cook for 4–5 minutes.
4. Add 1 dessertspoon flour, stir,
then add boiling water. Season to
taste with salt and pepper and
simmer for 12–13 minutes.
5. Add finely sliced mushrooms,
sherry and parsley. Blend in fish,
prawns or shrimps, reserving a
few for decoration.
6. Grease a large soufflé dish,
sprinkle sides and bottom with
some of the grated cheese and
pour in about a third of fish
mixture.
7. Melt 1oz (25gm) butter in a
saucepan, stir in 1oz (25gm) flour
and gradually add milk.
8. Remove pan from heat and beat
in egg yolks, one at a time. Reheat
until sauce begins to boil, stirring
constantly.
9. Beat in remaining cheese and
a pinch of paprika.
10. Beat egg whites until stiff and
fold gently into the sauce. Fill
soufflé dish with this mixture and
bake in centre of oven for 20–25
minutes.
11. Boil rice in plenty of boiling,
salted water for about 10 minutes
until tender. Drain well and press
into a ring mould.
12. Turn rice out carefully on to a
dish, fill centre with remaining
fish mixture and garnish with
prawns or shrimps and lemon
slices.
13. Serve very hot together with
the soufflé.

FISH AND MUSHROOM BAKE
Serves 4

1lb (½ kilo) white fish
½ onion or 2 sticks celery
2oz (50gm) mushrooms
1oz (25gm) butter
1 can condensed mushroom soup
2 tablespoons chopped parsley
salt and pepper
2lb (1 kilo) hot, mashed potato
1 tomato

1. Bring fish to boil in a covered pan of water, turn off heat and leave for 5 minutes.
2. Chop onion or celery and slice mushrooms, then fry in butter. Add soup.
3. Drain, skin and flake fish, and add it to the sauce, with parsley and seasoning.
4. When mixture is hot, pour it into an ovenware dish.
5. Pile hot potatoes over the fish. Slice tomato and arrange on the top.
6. Brown under grill and serve immediately.

FISH AND CHEESE SUPREME
Serves 4–6

6 or 8 thin slices buttered toast
8oz (200gm) freshly cooked white fish, flaked
8oz (200gm) mild cheese, grated
3 eggs
½ pint (250ml) single cream
½ pint (250ml) milk
salt, pepper and paprika pepper

1. Preheat oven to very moderate, 325 deg F or gas 3 (170 deg C).
2. Butter an ovenware dish. Line it with buttered toast and cover toast with flaked fish.
3. Sprinkle liberally with cheese.
4. Beat the eggs and mix with cream and milk. Pour into the dish.
5. Sprinkle with salt, pepper and paprika pepper.
6. Bake in centre of oven for about 50 minutes, until lightly set. Serve at once.

CHEESY FISH
Serves 4

1lb (½ kilo) cooked white fish
1oz (25gm) butter
1oz (25gm) flour
½ pint (250ml) milk
salt and pepper
2oz (50gm) cheese, grated
3 tomatoes, chopped
1lb (½ kilo) hot, mashed potato
1 egg, beaten

1. Preheat oven to moderately hot, 400 deg F or gas 6 (200 deg C).
2. Remove the skin and bones from the fish and flake it roughly with a fork.
3. Melt the butter in a pan and add flour. Cook for a minute and then gradually add the milk, stirring.
4. Bring to the boil and season.
5. Add most of the cheese.
6. Mix with the fish and pour into a shallow ovenware dish, together with the tomatoes.
7. Sprinkle with rest of cheese and bake for 30 minutes in centre of oven.
8. Surround with mashed potato. Brush potato with egg and grill lightly or return to the oven for a few minutes to brown.

FISH CHOWDER
Serves 4

2oz (50gm) bacon
2 onions, sliced
4 potatoes, sliced or diced
salt and pepper
1 pint (approximately ½ litre) boiling water
1lb (½ kilo) haddock or cod, fresh or smoked
1 pint (approximately ½ litre) milk
2oz (50gm) butter
grated cheese
1 teaspoon chopped parsley

1. Chop bacon coarsely and fry in a saucepan until golden brown. Remove and put on one side.
2. Cook onions in bacon fat until tender.
3. Add potatoes, salt, pepper, water and bacon.
4. Cut fish into chunks and place on top.
5. Cover pan and simmer until potatoes are cooked, then add milk and butter.
6. Serve topped with cheese and parsley.

SCALLOPED HADDOCK
Serves 4

8oz (200gm) smoked haddock
½ pint (250ml) milk
1 tablespoon chopped onion
1 blade of mace
1oz (25gm) butter
1oz (25gm) flour
salt and pepper
browned breadcrumbs
1lb (½ kilo) potato, creamed
watercress or parsley to garnish

1. Wash the fish and simmer gently in the milk with the onion and mace.
2. Remove the fish and flake it, then divide between four scallop shells or individual dishes.
3. Melt the butter, add the flour, then gradually add the milk, stirring all the time.
4. Bring to the boil and season well.
5. Pour the sauce over the fish, then sprinkle with breadcrumbs.
6. Pipe the potato all round the edge of the shells.
7. Put under the grill to heat through and brown the potato.
8. Garnish with watercress or parsley and serve.

NEPTUNE'S CASSEROLE
Serves 4

1lb (½ kilo) fresh haddock,
steamed
2 shallots, finely chopped
1 teaspoon finely chopped
parsley
1 can anchovies, finely
chopped
salt and pepper
juice of 1 lemon
1 wine glass white wine
1lb (½ kilo) tomatoes, skinned
white breadcrumbs
a little butter

1. Preheat oven to moderate, 350
deg F or gas 4 (180 deg C).
2. Skin, bone and flake the fish,
put in a deep, greased casserole
and press down.
3. Mix the shallots, parsley and
anchovies together in a bowl,
season and add lemon juice.
4. Add wine to mixture and
spread over the fish.
5. Cover with sliced tomatoes,
sprinkle with breadcrumbs and
dot with butter.
6. Cover and bake for 20–30
minutes.

HADDOCK CASSEROLE
Serves 4

1lb (½ kilo) fresh haddock
1 onion, chopped
1 can (4oz or 100gm) whole
French beans
4oz (100gm) cheese, grated
salt and pepper
1 small can tomatoes
3 large potatoes
parsley to garnish

1. Preheat oven to moderate, 350
deg F or gas 4 (180 deg C).
2. Skin fish and cut into cubes.
Place in a casserole.
3. Cover with onion, drained
beans and half the cheese. Season.
4. Add tomatoes, cover with
sliced potatoes and season again.
5. Bake in centre of oven for 1
hour.
6. Cover with remaining cheese
and put back in oven for a few
minutes until brown.
7. Garnish with parsley.

PROVENÇAL FISH PIE
Serves 4

1 onion, chopped
4 tomatoes, skinned and
chopped
4½oz (112gm) butter
1 tablespoon chopped parsley
juice of ½ lemon
⅓ pint (200ml) water
salt and pepper
½oz (12gm) cornflour
1lb (½ kilo) haddock or cod,
cooked and flaked
2oz (50gm) processed Gruyère
cheese, sieved
2oz (50gm) flour

1. Preheat oven to hot, 425 deg F
or gas 7 (220 deg C).
2. Cook onion and tomatoes in
2½oz (62gm) butter.
3. Add half the parsley, lemon
juice and half the water, season
and simmer for 5 minutes.
4. Blend the cornflour with
remaining water and stir into pan.
Cook for a further 5 minutes.
5. Stir in fish and cheese then
place in a pie dish.
6. Rub the remaining butter into
flour, add rest of parsley and
sprinkle over fish.
7. Bake in centre of oven for
15–20 minutes.

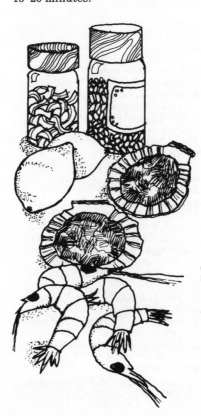

CREAMED HADDOCK WITH MUSHROOMS
Serves 4

2lb (1 kilo) fresh haddock,
filleted
1lb (½ kilo) mushrooms
1oz (25gm) onion, chopped and
parboiled
1 dessertspoon parsley,
chopped
2½oz (62gm) butter
¼ pint (125ml) water
4 tablespoons dry white wine
½oz (12gm) flour
¼ pint (125ml) hot milk
salt and pepper
juice of half lemon
paprika
4oz (100gm) cheese, grated
boiled potatoes
1 teaspoon parsley, chopped
sprigs of parsley to garnish

1. Preheat oven to hot, 450 deg F
or gas 8 (230 deg C).
2. Divide fish into four portions.
3. Wash mushrooms but do not
peel them. Reserve one large
mushroom and chop the rest
finely.
4. Mix with chopped onion and
parsley.
5. Melt 2oz (50gm) butter in a
saucepan, add mushroom and
onion mixture and cook gently
for 2–3 minutes.
6. Put fish in a shallow, ovenware
dish and pour water and wine
over.
7. Slice remaining mushroom and
sprinkle it in. Cover with a lid
or greased paper and cook in
centre of oven for 15 minutes.
8. When cooked, strain off liquor
and boil it in a pan for 7 minutes.
9. In another pan melt remaining
butter, add flour and pour on
gradually ¼ pint (125ml) reduced
liquor and the hot milk. Simmer
for 5 minutes and season to taste.
10. Stir in lemon juice, 1 teaspoon
paprika and half the cheese.
11. Stir about ¼ pint (125ml) sauce
into mushroom mixture and cover
the bottom of a shallow serving
dish with it.
12. Arrange fish on top and coat
with remaining sauce. Sprinkle
with remaining cheese.
13. Surround with boiled potatoes
sprinkled with parsley and
paprika.
14. Garnish with sprigs of parsley
and serve at once.

Gammon and orange (see page 28) Sausagemeat balls with Spanish rice (see page 64)

Mushrooms and kidneys in a dish (see page 67) Braised liver casserole with creamed potato (see page 65)

Fruited herrings (see page 38)   Fish curry with poppadoms (see page 31)

Cod with grapes (see page 30)   Sole mornay (see page 43)

SEAFOOD PIE
Serves 4

1lb ($\frac{1}{2}$ kilo) fresh haddock
1$\frac{1}{2}$ pints (approximately $\frac{3}{4}$ litre)
water
$\frac{1}{2}$ small onion
salt and pepper
1 small can lobster meat,
broken into pieces
2oz (50gm) prawns, shelled
$\frac{1}{2}$ small packet frozen peas or
4oz (100gm) fresh peas
juice of $\frac{1}{2}$ lemon
$\frac{1}{2}$oz (12gm) butter
$\frac{1}{2}$oz (12gm) flour
$\frac{1}{4}$ pint (125ml) dry cider
1 packet (8oz or 200gm) frozen
puff pastry, thawed (or see
Basic recipes, page 100)

1. Preheat oven to hot, 425 deg F
or gas 7 (220 deg C).
2. Skin the haddock and poach it
for 10 minutes in water with fish
skin, sliced onion and seasoning.
3. Drain fish, reserving the fish
stock. Flake the fish into large
pieces.
4. Put into a bowl with lobster
meat, prawns and peas.
5. Sprinkle with lemon juice.
6. Melt the butter in a pan, mix
in the flour and cook gently for 1
minute.
7. Remove from the heat and
whisk in the cider and a scant $\frac{1}{4}$
pint (125ml) strained fish stock.
8. Simmer, stirring well, for 2
minutes.
9. Pour over fish mixture and
spoon into a 1$\frac{1}{2}$-pint
(approximately $\frac{3}{4}$ litre) pie dish.
Allow to cool.
10. Roll out pastry thinly to
1 inch bigger than the top of the
pie dish.
11. Trim off this extra inch, damp
it and stick round the rim of the
dish.
12. Top with remaining pastry.
Neaten the edge and decorate
with pastry leaves.
13. Bake in the centre of oven for
30 minutes, or until the pastry is
risen and golden brown.

HADDOCK VOL AU VENT
Serves 6

8oz (200gm) boiled fresh
haddock
$\frac{1}{2}$oz (12gm) butter
$\frac{1}{2}$oz (12gm) flour
$\frac{1}{4}$ pint (125ml) milk
2oz (50gm) mushrooms, sliced
1 wineglass dry white wine
2 egg yolks
salt and pepper
6 bought vol au vent pastry
cases
chopped parsley

1. Flake the fish.
2. Melt butter in a pan and stir
in the flour. Add milk gradually,
stirring constantly.
3. Boil mushrooms for 2 minutes
in wine and add to white sauce.
4. Fold in egg yolks and seasoning
and reheat the fish in this
mixture.
5. Fill pastry cases with mixture
and sprinkle tops with chopped
parsley.

CREAMED HALIBUT WITH MUSHROOMS
Serves 6

6 half halibut steaks, $\frac{3}{4}$ inch
thick
2oz (50gm) butter
2oz (50gm) flour
1 pint (approximately $\frac{1}{2}$ litre)
milk
4 tablespoons white wine
5 mushrooms, sliced
4 tablespoons cream
salt and pepper

1. Preheat oven to moderate to
moderately hot, 375 deg F or gas 5
(190 deg C).
2. Trim the steaks and arrange on
four pieces of foil, large enough to
wrap up fish.
3. Melt the butter, add the flour
and cook gently for 2–3 minutes.
4. Stir in the milk, bring to the
boil and add the wine and
mushrooms.
5. Cook for a further 3–4 minutes,
stirring continuously.
6. Remove from the heat and stir
in the cream. Season to taste.
7. Divide the sauce over the
steaks and seal in the foil,
twisting the ends securely.
8. Place in a baking dish and
cook in centre of oven for 30
minutes.
9. Serve on a hot dish.

FILLET OF HALIBUT MARIE-ROSE
Serves 4–6

3 large halibut steaks
6oz (150gm) butter
2oz (50gm) shallots or onions,
chopped
4oz (100gm) mushrooms
salt and pepper
$\frac{1}{2}$ bottle dry cider
2 lemons
1 bayleaf
1 sprig of thyme or a pinch of
dried thyme
1 small stick celery
2lb (1 kilo) small, preferably
new, potatoes
1oz (25gm) flour
$\frac{1}{2}$ pint (250ml) milk
paprika
1 teaspoon tomato purée or
ketchup
2 egg yolks
chopped parsley

1. Preheat oven to hot, 425 deg F
or gas 7 (220 deg C).
2. Place skinned fish in a shallow,
ovenware dish greased with half
the butter.
3. Sprinkle the dish with onion
and sliced mushroom stalks,
reserving the heads for
garnishing.
4. Lay fish on top, sprinkle with
salt and pepper and cover with
cider and lemon juice.
5. Add bayleaf, thyme and celery,
dot with 2oz (50gm) butter cut
into small pieces and bake in
centre of oven for 15–20 minutes.
6. When cooked, remove the
bones and keep warm.
7. Boil the potatoes.
8. Strain liquor in which fish was
cooked and boil for 5 minutes.
9. Melt remaining butter in a pan,
stir in flour and gradually add
reduced fish liquor and the milk,
stirring constantly.
10. Season to taste, then divide
into two equal parts. To one add
paprika and tomato purée or
ketchup and simmer for a further
5 minutes.
11. To the other add egg yolks,
bring gently to the boil and
remove from the heat.
12. Divide halibut steaks and
arrange on a large serving dish.
Coat them alternatively with red
and yellow sauces.
13. Group the potatoes between
the fish and garnish with lightly
fried mushroom heads and
parsley.

BALINESE HERRINGS
Serves 4

2 tablespoons cooking oil
2 medium onions
2 garlic cloves
¼ teaspoon powdered ginger
2 tablespoons soy sauce
2 teaspoons sugar
juice of 1 lemon
2 cans herring fillets in
tomato-chilli sauce
½ pint (250ml) water

1. Heat oil in frying pan.
2. Slice the onion thinly into
rings and fry until transparent.
3. Add crushed garlic, ginger, soy
sauce, sugar and lemon juice.
4. Open can of herring fillets and
add to pan. Rinse can out with
water, adding this to the pan.
5. Heat herrings gently in sauce.
6. Serve immediately with fried or
boiled rice.

HERRINGS PICCALO
Serves 4

4 whole herrings, boned and
cleaned
½ pint (250ml) milk
2 heaped tablespoons piccalilli
1oz (25gm) butter
1oz (25gm) flour
1 carton soured cream
lemon slices to garnish

1. Preheat oven to moderate to
moderately hot, 375 deg F or gas 5
(190 deg C).
2. Cut herrings down back,
making two fillets.
3. From the tail-end, roll fillets up
with skin side inside.
4. Place upright with cut side on
bottom of an ovenware dish.
5. Pour milk over mixed with
piccalilli.
6. Cover with foil and bake in
centre of oven for 20 minutes.
7. Remove herrings carefully,
place on a serving dish and keep
hot. Reserve liquor from cooking.
8. Melt butter in saucepan, stir in
flour and cook for 2–3 minutes.
9. Remove from heat and
gradually stir in liquor.
10. Return to heat, bring to boil
and cook 2–3 minutes, stirring
continuously.
11. Add soured cream.
12. Pour sauce over herrings and
garnish each fillet with a lemon
butterfly.

BAKED HERRING SUPPER DISH
Serves 4

4 herrings
salt and pepper
1lb (½ kilo) tomatoes
4oz (100gm) small onions
1 tablespoon oil
1 teaspoon sugar
pinch of salt
freshly ground black pepper
2 tablespoons wine vinegar
1 level tablespoon French
mustard
½oz (12gm) butter, melted
1 teaspoon roughly chopped
parsley

1. Preheat oven to moderate to
moderately hot, 375 deg F or gas 5
(190 deg C).
2. Butter an ovenware dish.
3. Trim and clean herrings. Score
on each side with a sharp knife
and season well.
4. Skin and cut tomatoes into
wedges.
5. Skin onions, slice them thinly,
then cook until tender in the oil.
6. Put the tomatoes and onions in
the bottom of the dish and
sprinkle with sugar, salt and
plenty of black pepper.
7. Pour vinegar over, blended
with mustard, and arrange
herrings on top.
8. Brush with melted butter.
9. Cover with foil or a lid and
bake in centre of oven for 30
minutes. Remove lid or foil and
cook for a further 15 minutes.
10. Sprinkle with parsley to serve.

FRUITED HERRINGS
(Illustrated on page 36)
Serves 4

4 herrings
salt
Tabasco sauce
2oz (50gm) butter, melted
paprika pepper
1 grapefruit
1 orange
2 tomatoes
watercress to garnish

1. Score fish with a knife, then
place it on aluminium foil in grill
pan.
2. Sprinkle with salt and Tabasco
sauce. Pour half the fat over and
sprinkle with paprika pepper.
3. Grill until fish is cooked,
allowing 5–6 minutes on each side
for whole fish.
4. Arrange fish on a hot serving
dish, pour remaining fat over.
5. Garnish with half slices of
grapefruit, orange and tomato
and top with watercress sprigs.

FLORENTINE HERRINGS
Serves 4

½oz (12gm) butter
1 medium onion, finely chopped
2 packets (11oz or 275gm each)
frozen, chopped or leaf spinach
2 tablespoons cream
1 level teaspoon salt
pepper
4 whole herrings, boned
2oz (50gm) cheese, grated

1. Preheat oven to moderate to
moderately hot, 375 deg F or gas 5
(190 deg C).
2. Melt butter in large saucepan
with tightly fitting lid.
3. Add onion and cook gently
without colouring for 2–3 minutes.
4. Add spinach, cover with lid and
cook over moderate heat until
soft, about 3–4 minutes.
5. Remove lid and stir
continuously over fast heat to
cook off all the moisture. Stir in
cream and season well.
6. Spoon over base of large
shallow, ovenware dish.
7. Trim heads, tails and fins off
cleaned herrings.
8. Place diagonally on top of
spinach and sprinkle with cheese.
9. Bake in centre of oven for 25
minutes. Serve immediately.

STUFFED SOUSED HERRING
Serves 4

4 medium herrings
1 tomato, skinned and chopped
2oz (50gm) boiled rice, seasoned
with salt and pepper (raw
weight)
¼ pint (125ml) malt vinegar
¼ pint (125ml) water
1 blade of mace
2 cloves
½ bayleaf
pinch of salt
1 onion

1. Preheat oven to moderate,
350 deg F or gas 4 (180 deg C).
2. Wash, trim and bone the fish,
keeping them whole.
3. Mix tomato with rice and
spread rice mixture on cut sides
of herrings.
4. Fold herrings in half, heads to
tails, and put in a pie dish.
5. Cover with vinegar and water
and add mace, cloves, bayleaf,
salt and sliced onion.
6. Cover with foil or greaseproof
paper and bake in centre of oven
for 1 hour. Remove from oven and
leave to cool.

ANDALUSIAN HERRINGS
Serves 4

4 large herrings
1 medium onion, finely chopped
1oz (25gm) butter
4 tomatoes, roughly chopped
2 teaspoons tomato purée
4 tablespoons vinegar
¼ pint (125ml) water
1 teaspoon flour
1 garlic clove
salt and pepper

1. Preheat oven to moderate, 350
deg F or gas 4 (180 deg C).
2. Clean and fillet the herrings.
3. Cut each fillet into two and roll
up, skin side out. Stand them
upright in a buttered casserole.
4. Fry the onion lightly in the
butter.
5. Add tomatoes, tomato purée,
vinegar, water, the flour blended
with a little cold water, and
crushed garlic.
6. Season well with salt and
pepper and pour this sauce over
the herrings.
7. Bake in centre of oven for 30
minutes.

HERRING-STUFFED POTATOES
Serves 4

4 old potatoes
1 level teaspoon salt
4 herrings, boned
2oz (50gm) butter
1 carton soured cream

1. Preheat oven to moderate to
moderately hot, 375 deg F or gas 5
(190 deg C).
2. Scrub potatoes, prick
thoroughly, place in roasting tin
and sprinkle with salt.
3. Bake on bottom shelf of oven
for 1–1½ hours, until skewer
passes through them easily.
4. Wrap herrings in foil and top
each with a knob of butter 30
minutes before potatoes are
cooked.
5. Bake at top of oven for 20
minutes.
6. Remove herrings and potatoes
from oven and increase setting to
hot, 425 deg F or gas 7 (220 deg C)
7. Slit top of each potato and
scoop out the inside. Mash with
rest of butter and season.
8. Drain any excess butter from
herrings and add to potatoes.
9. Skin herrings, mash flesh well
and add to potatoes.
10. Pile herring mixture into
potato jackets and spoon soured
cream over each.
11. Place on serving dish and
return to the oven, until piping
hot.

DEEP SEA QUICHE
Serves 4

shortcrust pastry made with
6oz (150gm) flour (see Basic
recipes, page 100)
2 eggs
¼ pint (125ml) milk
2 spring onions, finely chopped
salt and pepper
1 can herring fillets
1oz (25gm) butter

1. Preheat oven to moderately
hot, 400 deg F or gas 6 (200 deg C).
2. Roll out pastry to fit an 8-inch
(20cm) flan case or ring.
3. Prick base and line with
greaseproof paper. Fill with
baking beans and bake for 10
minutes.
4. Remove beans. Turn down oven
heat to 350 deg F or gas 4 (180 deg
C) and bake for a further 10
minutes.
5. Beat eggs with milk, then add
spring onions and salt and pepper.
6. Arrange herring fillets in base
of flan case.
7. Pour egg mixture over herrings
and dot with nuts of butter.
8. Return to centre of oven for 35
minutes until puffed and golden.
9. Serve hot or cold with tossed
green salad.

HERRING ROE RAMEKINS
Serves 4

1 can herring roes, drained
1 can condensed cream of
mushroom soup
1 carton (5oz or 125gm) soured
cream
salt and pepper
2oz (50gm) butter
2oz (50gm) fresh, white
breadcrumbs
2 tablespoons chopped parsley

1. Preheat oven to moderate, 350
deg F or gas 4 (180 deg C).
2. Divide herring roes between
four small heatproof dishes or
ramekins.
3. Combine mushroom soup with
soured cream and season. Spoon
over roes.
4. Melt butter in a pan, add the
breadcrumbs and toss until well
coated.
5. Add parsley and mix well.
6. Sprinkle over the ramekins and
bake for 15–20 minutes, until the
crumbs are lightly browned.

SAVOURY ROE CRUMBLE
Serves 4

1 can soft herring roes
2 eggs
1 level teaspoon salt
pepper to taste
4oz (100gm) white breadcrumbs
1 tablespoon finely chopped
parsley
2oz (50gm) cheese, grated

1. Preheat oven to moderate to
moderately hot, 375 deg F or gas
5 (190 deg C).
2. Drain herring roes and place in
bottom of flameproof dish.
3. Beat eggs thoroughly with salt
and pepper and pour over roes.
4. Mix together breadcrumbs,
parsley and cheese. Spread evenly
over roe and egg mixture.
5. Bake in centre of oven for 20–
25 minutes.
6. Place dish under hot grill to
brown topping.

LEMON-STUFFED
HERRINGS IN CREAMY
MUSHROOM SAUCE
Serves 4

4 herrings
2oz (50gm) butter
1 medium onion, finely chopped
3 slices white bread, crumbed
grated rind and juice of 1 lemon
1 tablespoon chopped parsley
salt and pepper
2 tablespoons water
2oz (50gm) mushrooms, sliced
1 carton soured cream

1. Preheat oven to moderate, 350
deg F or gas 4 (180 deg C).
2. Scale, clean and bone herrings.
3. Melt half the butter in a frying
pan and gently cook onion until
tender.
4. Add to breadcrumbs in a basin.
5. Stir in rind of lemon and
parsley. Season to taste.
6. Divide into four and fill the
centre of each herring.
7. Place herrings side by side in a
greased, ovenware casserole.
8. Pour lemon juice over, mixed
with water and add the
mushrooms.
9. Dot with remaining butter.
Cover and bake for 30 minutes.
10. Just before serving, stir in the
soured cream.

STUFFED HERRING
CASSEROLE
Serves 4

4 herrings
2oz (50gm) breadcrumbs
1 small onion, finely chopped
1 teaspoon chopped parsley
pinch of mixed herbs
salt and pepper
½oz (12gm) butter
1 packet (1 pint or
approximately ½ litre) tomato
soup mix
1 pint (approximately ½ litre)
water

1. Preheat oven to moderate, 350
deg F or gas 4 (180 deg C).
2. Clean and bone the herrings.
3. Mix together the breadcrumbs,
onion, parsley, mixed herbs,
seasoning and butter.
4. Stuff the herrings and secure
each fish with a skewer.
5. Arrange them in a greased
casserole.
6. Mix tomato soup with hot
water and bring to the boil. Whisk
well.
7. Pour over herrings and bake
for about 20 minutes.
8. Serve hot.

KIPPER CROQUETTES
Serves 4

2 packets frozen kipper fillets
1 packet (5–6 servings) instant
mashed potato powder
1 egg, separated
salt and pepper
2 teaspoons lemon juice
breadcrumbs for coating
oil for frying
lemon twists and parsley sprigs
to garnish

1. Cook kipper fillets according to
instructions on packet.
2. Drain fillets, remove skin and
flake flesh finely.
3. Make up potato according to
instructions on packet.
4. Stir in egg yolk and flaked
kipper, season well and add
lemon juice. Leave to cool.
5. Form into 12 croquettes, about
4 inches long.
6. Beat egg white with 2
tablespoons water and dip each
croquette in it. Coat in
breadcrumbs.
7. Chill well before frying in
shallow or deep fat, until crisp
and golden. Drain on absorbent
paper.
8. Serve hot, garnished with
lemon twists and sprigs of parsley.

KIPPER CAKES
Serves 4

8oz (200gm) kipper fillets,
cooked
8oz (200gm) mashed potato
1oz (25gm) butter
2 eggs, beaten
1 teaspoon chopped parsley
salt and pepper
2 tablespoons browned
breadcrumbs
fat or oil for frying
lemon slices and parsley to
garnish

1. Mix together the flaked kipper,
potato, butter, half the beaten egg
and parsley.
2. Season well with pepper and a
little salt, if required.
3. Divide mixture into six and
mould into round cakes.
4. Coat the cakes with rest of egg
and breadcrumbs.
5. Fry in hot fat or oil on both
sides until golden brown.
6. Drain and garnish with lemon
and parsley.

APPLE-STUFFED KIPPERS
Serves 4

2 pairs kippers
4oz (100gm) button mushrooms
1oz (25gm) butter
4oz (100gm) tomatoes
1 apple, cored
juice of ½ lemon

1. Preheat oven to hot, 425 deg F or gas 7 (220 deg C).
2. Carefully remove large bones from kippers.
3. Fold in half and place, with tails uppermost, down centre of ovenware dish.
4. Pull tails back, so that kippers are opened ready for filling.
5. Cut mushrooms into quarters.
6. Melt butter in a saucepan, add mushrooms and toss over heat for a few seconds.
7. Cut tomatoes and apples into ½-inch pieces, add to mushrooms and mix well. Add lemon juice.
8. Fill kippers with this mixture, folding the tails over again.
9. Cover with foil and bake for 20–25 minutes. Serve at once.

KIPPER CHEESE PIE
Serves 4

1 packet boil-in-the-bag kipper fillets
4oz (100gm) cheese, grated
salt and pepper
1 packet (11oz or 275gm) frozen puff pastry, thawed (or see Basic recipes, page 100)
1 egg, beaten

1. Preheat oven to hot, 425 deg F or gas 7 (220 deg C).
2. Cook kippers according to directions on the packet.
3. Remove kippers from bag and place in a large bowl.
4. While still hot, mash thoroughly and stir in cheese. Season to taste and leave to cool.
5. Roll out pastry to a long strip, 8 inches by 24 inches and cut into two.
6. Place one piece of pastry on a baking sheet and spread with the kipper filling, leaving a ½ inch border.
7. Damp edges with water and cover with the second piece of pastry, sealing the edges well.
8. Cut two or three slits in the top. Brush with egg.
9. Bake in oven on the second shelf down for 15 minutes.

STUFFED MACKEREL
Serves 4

4 mackerel
1oz (25gm) suet
1oz (25gm) ham or bacon
2oz (50gm) breadcrumbs
1 teaspoon chopped parsley
pinch of mixed herbs
grated rind of half lemon
salt and pepper
1 egg, beaten
butter to baste

1. Preheat oven to moderate, 350 deg F or gas 4 (180 deg C).
2. Cut off the heads and tails of the fish. Clean and remove the roe and take out the backbone.
3. Mix together suet, ham or bacon, breadcrumbs, parsley, mixed herbs, lemon rind, salt and pepper and bind with egg.
4. Stuff the fish with the mixture, lay them in a greased dish and cook in centre of oven for 40 minutes.
5. Baste well with butter during the cooking.

CURLED WHITING
Serves 4

4 whiting
2 eggs, beaten
2oz (50gm) browned crumbs
deep fat for frying
parsley and lemon twists to garnish

1. Clean the fish but do not cut off the head. Remove the eyes.
2. Skin the whiting by slitting the skin down the back with a sharp knife and cutting it round the tail-end of the fish. Put some salt on your fingers and pull off the fish skin.
3. Dip the fish in egg and coat with breadcrumbs.
4. Take the tail of each fish and push through the eye sockets.
5. Fry in deep fat for about 4 minutes. Drain on absorbent paper.
6. Serve garnished with sprigs of parsley and lemon twists.

CURRIED FILLETS OF FISH
Serves 4

1½oz (37gm) dripping
1 onion
1 sharp-flavoured apple
1 tablespoon curry powder
1 teaspoon curry paste
1½oz (37gm) flour
¾ pint (375ml) fish stock or water
salt and pepper
a little sugar
chutney
6 plaice or haddock fillets
6oz (150gm) long-grain rice
lemon and parsley to garnish

1. Preheat oven to moderate to moderately hot, 375 deg F or gas 5 (190 deg C).
2. Melt the dripping in a pan and fry the chopped onion.
3. Peel and chop the apple, add to the pan and cook for several minutes.
4. Add the curry powder and paste and cook for a further 5 minutes, then add the flour and cook for several more minutes.
5. Pour in the stock or water gradually.
6. Add the seasoning, sugar and chutney to taste.
7. Roll up the fish fillets and put them into a casserole dish, pour on the curry sauce and cook in centre of oven for 30 minutes.
8. Meanwhile, boil the rice in fast boiling, salted, water for 10–15 minutes, drain well and dry it off.
9. Serve the curry garnished with lemon and tiny sprigs of parsley and accompanied by rice.

PLAICE WITH CREAMED MUSHROOM SAUCE
Serves 4

2 packets boneless whole plaice
3oz (75gm) butter or margarine
4oz (100gm) button mushrooms, thinly sliced
1 can cream
4 teaspoons lemon juice
4 teaspoons chopped parsley
salt and pepper
parsley sprigs to garnish

1. Put the plaice on the grill rack. Dot with 1oz (25gm) butter or margarine and grill under a low heat for 5 minutes.
2. Turn carefully, dot the fish with another 1oz (25gm) butter and grill until cooked.
3. Melt 1oz (25gm) butter or margarine in a small saucepan and fry the mushrooms until tender.
4. Add the cream, lemon juice and parsley, season to taste and reheat, but do not boil.
5. Serve the plaice on a hot dish with the sauce spooned over. Garnish with parsley sprigs.

PLAICE A LA CREME
Serves 2–4

4 plaice fillets
salt and pepper
1 small bayleaf
4oz (100gm) button mushrooms
1½oz (37gm) butter
1 packet Hollandaise sauce
½ pint (250ml) milk
1 lemon

1. Place fillets in a pan with water just to cover. Season with salt, pepper and bayleaf, cover and simmer for 3–5 minutes, until fish is tender. Strain fish and keep hot.
2. Slice mushrooms and fry in hot butter for 2 minutes.
3. Prepare sauce, following directions on packet, using milk. Season with salt, pepper and juice of half lemon.
4. Stir mushrooms into sauce.
5. Place fish on a serving dish and pour sauce over.
6. Cut remaining half lemon into wedges and place round edge of dish.

FILLETS OF PLAICE WITH BLACK BUTTER
Serves 4

8 plaice fillets
juice of 1 lemon
salt and pepper
2oz (50gm) unsalted butter
1½ tablespoons vinegar
2 teaspoons finely chopped parsley
2–3 gherkins, chopped

1. Preheat oven to moderate to moderately hot, 375 deg F or gas 5 (190 deg C).
2. Sprinkle the fillets with some of the lemon juice and seasoning.
3. Fold each fillet in three and put in a buttered dish. Pour the rest of the lemon juice over them.
4. Cover with well-buttered paper and cook in centre of oven for 10–15 minutes.
5. Meanwhile, cut the butter into small pieces and put in a small, strong pan.
6. Heat until it is a golden brown, then take off the heat at once and leave to cool.
7. Put the vinegar in another small pan and reduce it to about half the original quantity.
8. Stir in the butter and reheat. Season and add the parsley.
9. Pour the black butter over the fish and sprinkle with gherkins.

PLAICE WITH PINEAPPLE AND MUSHROOMS
Serves 4

4 large plaice fillets
1 egg, beaten
2oz (50gm) white breadcrumbs
fat for frying
4 canned pineapple rings
4 large mushrooms
2–3 gherkins, sliced
1oz (25gm) butter

1. Coat the plaice fillets in egg and breadcrumbs and fry in shallow fat until golden
2. Drain and put into a hot serving dish.
3. Simmer the pineapple in a little of the juice.
4. Lightly fry the mushrooms and gherkins in butter.
5. Place a pineapple ring on each of the plaice fillets.
6. Top with a mushroom and sprinkle with the sliced gherkins.

PLAICE AND ORANGES
Serves 4

2 oranges
8 plaice fillets
1oz (25gm) flour, seasoned with salt and pepper
2oz (50gm) butter
1 teaspoon mixed chopped herbs
1 teaspoon lemon juice

1. Peel and remove the pith from the oranges. Cut into thin slices crossways.
2. Heat in a pan with a little water.
3. Skin the fillets, then wash and dry thoroughly. Coat with seasoned flour.
4. Heat a heavy frying pan and add half the butter. Put in the fillets with the skinned side uppermost. Cook over a moderate heat until just golden on both sides.
5. Put the fish in a hot dish overlapping the fillets slightly.
6. Garnish with the oranges and keep hot.
7. Add the rest of the butter to a clean pan. Heat and allow to colour a nut brown.
8. Stir in the mixed herbs and lemon juice.
9. Pour over the fish and serve at once.

PORTUGUESE PLAICE
Serves 4

1 tablespoon chopped chives
3 tomatoes, skinned and sliced
1oz (25gm) butter
8 plaice fillets
a little white wine
salt and pepper

1. Preheat oven to moderate, 350 deg F or gas 4 (180 deg C).
2. Fry chives and tomatoes in butter for a few minutes, then pour into a fireproof dish.
3. Fold each fillet in three and lay them on the tomatoes.
4. Cover the tomatoes and fish with wine. Add salt and pepper.
5. Bake in centre of oven for 25 minutes.

FISH AND TOMATO CASSEROLE
Serves 4

8 plaice fillets
salt and pepper
5oz (125gm) cheese, grated
1oz (25gm) butter
1oz (25gm) flour
½ pint (250ml) milk
8oz (200gm) tomatoes, skinned

1. Preheat oven to moderate to moderately hot, 375 deg F or gas 5 (190 deg C).
2. Fold the fillets in half.
3. Sprinkle with salt and pepper and put in a casserole.
4. Cover with 2oz (50gm) cheese.
5. Bake in centre of oven for 10–15 minutes, until the fish is cooked.
6. Meanwhile, melt butter, add flour and cook for 1–2 minutes.
7. Gradually add milk and bring to the boil, stirring all the time.
8. Add 1oz (25gm) cheese.
9. Cut up the tomatoes and add to the sauce. Season well.
10. Allow to cook slowly for about 5 minutes, then pour over the fish.
11. Cover with rest of cheese and grill until golden brown.

SOLE WITH MUSHROOM CREAM SAUCE
Serves 4

8 sole fillets
4 level teaspoons mild mustard
1 can cream of mushroom soup
¼ pint (125ml) milk
few whole mushrooms, cooked
1oz (25gm) butter
1lb (½ kilo) hot, mashed potato
salt and pepper

1. Preheat oven to moderate to moderately hot, 375 deg F or gas 5 (190 deg C).
2. Skin, trim and wash fillets.
3. Spread with half the mild mustard and roll up. Place in a greased ovenware dish.
4. Blend soup with 2 tablespoons milk and pour over the sole. Scatter with mushrooms. Cover with foil or a lid.
5. Heat rest of milk with the butter and add to potatoes. Beat until smooth and creamy.
6. Add the rest of the mustard.
7. Season to taste and pipe into swirls on a greased baking tin.
8. Bake fish on the centre shelf and potatoes on the second shelf from the top of oven for 20 minutes.
9. Serve fish surrounded with the potatoes.

SOLE MORNAY
(Illustrated on page 36)
Serves 4

2 Dover sole
juice of ½ lemon
½ pint (250ml) fish stock (make from fish bones and skin)
8oz (200gm) hot, mashed potato
2oz (50gm) butter
1 egg, beaten
1oz (25gm) flour
4oz (100gm) cheese, grated
salt and pepper
sprigs of parsley
slices of lemon

1. Preheat oven to moderate, 350 deg F or gas 4 (180 deg C).
2. Wash, skin and fillet the sole.
3. Put the fillets in a buttered ovenware dish, folding each in half.
4. Add the lemon juice and the fish stock.
5. Cover the dish with foil or buttered greaseproof paper.
6. Cook on centre shelf of oven for 10 minutes.
7. Strain stock into a basin and keep the fish hot.
8. Cream the potato with 1oz (25gm) butter and half the beaten egg. Pipe it in rosettes round the edge of a fireproof dish.
9. Brush potato gently with the rest of the egg.
10. Heat the remaining butter, add the flour and gradually beat in the strained fish stock.
11. Cook until the sauce will coat the back of a spoon. Stir in 3oz (75gm) cheese and season well with salt and pepper.
12. Place the fish in the centre of the piped potato.
13. Reheat the sauce and pour over the sole.
14. Sprinkle with rest of cheese and glaze lightly under the grill.
15. Garnish with parsley and lemon slices and serve immediately.

SHRIMP BAKE
Serves 4

1 large can new potatoes
½ pint (250ml) peeled shrimps
2 hard-boiled eggs, sliced
2oz (50gm) fresh breadcrumbs
¼ pint (125ml) single cream
2oz (50gm) butter
1 teaspoon chopped parsley

1. Preheat oven to moderately hot, 400 deg F or gas 6 (200 deg C).
2. Drain and slice the potatoes. Place in a buttered pie dish.
3. Cover with the shrimps, eggs and breadcrumbs.
4. Pour the cream over the top and dot with butter.
5. Bake in centre of oven for 15–20 minutes.
6. Sprinkle with parsley just before serving.

SHRIMP SCALLOPS
Serves 4

4oz (100gm) patna rice
1oz (25gm) butter
1oz (25gm) flour
1 can (10oz or 250gm) cream of chicken soup
2–4oz (50–100gm) shrimps
6 stuffed olives, sliced
1 tablespoon green pepper, diced and lightly fried

1. Cook rice in boiling, salted water for 10–15 minutes until tender. Rinse through with hot water and drain.
2. Melt butter in a pan, stir in flour, remove from heat and slowly add soup, stirring all the time.
3. Bring to the boil and simmer for 3 minutes.
4. Add shrimps, olives and pepper.
5. Divide the rice into four scallop shells, leaving a hollow in the centre.
6. Pour shrimp mixture into the middle and serve piping hot.

HOT CREAMED SHRIMPS AND RICE
Serves 4

2 small onions
1oz (25gm) butter
8oz (200gm) potted shrimps
2 level tablespoons flour
¼ pint (125ml) dry cider
1 dessertspoon mild mustard
salt and pepper
¼ pint (125ml) double cream
1 tablespoon chopped parsley

1. Finely chop the onions and gently fry them in butter until tender.
2. Add shrimps and allow butter to melt.
3. Stir in flour and cook for a few minutes.
4. Blend in cider, stirring well. Add mustard, salt and pepper. Remove from the heat.
5. Stir in cream and parsley.
6. Serve with boiled rice mixed with cooked peas.

SHRIMP MIX-UP
Serves 4

1 large onion
½oz (12gm) butter
¼ pint (125ml) boiling water
3 medium potatoes, sliced
salt and pepper
2 packets frozen shrimps or prawns or 1 pint (approximately ½ litre) fresh ones, shelled
4 tablespoons single cream
2oz (50gm) cheese, grated
1 teaspoon chopped parsley

1. Chop the onion and cook in hot butter for a few minutes, until tender but not brown.
2. Add water, potatoes and salt and pepper.
3. Cover and simmer gently for about 15 minutes, or until the potatoes are tender.
4. Add shrimps or prawns and cream and bring just to the boil.
5. Stir in the cheese and parsley.

PRAWN CURRY
Serves 4

2 medium onions
1oz (25gm) butter
2 teaspoons curry powder
1 tablespoon flour
1 garlic clove
scant ½ pint (250ml) stock or coconut milk
salt and cayenne pepper
1 tablespoon chutney
2 teaspoons lemon juice
2 teaspoons sugar
1 tablespoon cream
2 packets frozen prawns or 1 pint (approximately ½ litre) fresh ones, shelled

1. Chop the onions and fry in the butter.
2. Add curry powder and flour.
3. Cook for about 2 minutes then add chopped garlic and stock or milk.
4. Add seasonings, chutney, lemon juice and sugar, and simmer for 30–40 minutes.
5. Add the cream and most of the prawns. Reserve some for garnish.
6. Serve surrounded by a border of boiled rice and garnished with whole prawns.

PRAWNS INDIENNE
Serves 4–6

2 onions, sliced
2 tablespoons cooking oil
1oz (25gm) flour
2 teaspoons curry powder
scant ½ pint (scant 250ml) water
salt and pepper
2oz (50gm) seedless raisins
2 cloves
juice and grated rind of 1 lemon
1 pint (approximately ½ litre) shelled prawns
red pepper to garnish

1. Fry onions in hot oil until tender, but not brown.
2. Blend in flour and curry powder.
3. Add water gradually and stir until it thickens.
4. Season well and add raisins, cloves, lemon juice and rind, and prawns.
5. Simmer for 10 minutes.
6. Serve piping hot, garnished with shreds of red pepper.

SCAMPI SUPPER
Serves 4

2 small onions
½oz (12gm) dripping
1 bacon rasher
8oz (200gm) tomatoes
½oz (12gm) flour
¼ pint (125ml) stock or water
salt and pepper
8oz (200gm) shelled scampi

1. Chop the onions, then fry them in the dripping until they are just starting to turn a light brown.
2. Add the chopped bacon and tomatoes and continue frying for about 1 minute.
3. Add flour and stock or water, bring to the boil and cook over a low heat for 5–10 minutes, then sieve.
4. Season well and add the scampi.
5. Cook through gently and serve with brown bread and butter.

DEVILLED CRAB FLAN
Serves 4–6

shortcrust pastry made with 6oz (150gm) flour (see Basic recipes, page 100)
salt
2 eggs
1 shallot, finely chopped and fried in a little butter
1 small can crab, well drained
¼ pint (125ml) single cream
black pepper
2 level teaspoons mustard
watercress to garnish

1. Preheat oven to hot, 425 deg F or gas 7 (220 deg C).
2. Roll out pastry and line a greased 8-inch (20cm) flan ring or sandwich tin. Prick base and chill.
3. Line with greaseproof paper and add some baking beans.
4. Bake in centre of oven for 15 minutes.
5. Remove paper and beans from flan. Turn oven heat down to moderate, 350 deg F or gas 4 (180 deg C).
6. Blend eggs in a bowl. Stir in all other ingredients.
7. Pour into flan case and bake in centre of oven until set.
8. Leave to cool slightly before removing flan ring.
9. Serve either hot or cold garnished with watercress.

CURRIED CRAB
Serves 4

1 onion
2oz (50gm) dripping
1 small apple
1 dessertspoon curry powder
1 tablespoon flour
1 can crab
½ pint (250ml) stock
salt and pepper
6oz (150gm) long-grain rice

1. Slice the onion and fry in the melted fat.
2. Add the chopped apple. Sprinkle with curry powder and cook for several minutes.
3. Add flour, the liquid drained from the crab and stock.
4. Season well, add the cut-up crab and heat.
5. Meanwhile, cook the rice in boiling, salted water for 10–15 minutes. Drain, rinse and dry.
6. Dish up the curry and surround with rice.

SCALLOPS MORNAY
Serves 4

4 scallops (make sure shells are firmly closed)
1 tablespoon lemon juice
2oz (50gm) butter
1oz (25gm) flour
½ pint (250ml) milk
4oz (100gm) petite Gruyère cheese, sieved
2oz (50gm) white breadcrumbs

1. To open the shells, place the scallops in a very moderate oven, 325 deg F or gas 3 (170 deg C).
2. Remove the black part and gristly fibre, leaving the red coral intact.
3. Cook in salted water with lemon juice for 10 minutes.
4. Clean the rounded shells.
5. Make the mornay sauce by melting the butter, adding the flour and cooking for a moment before whisking in the milk. Cook until the sauce coats the back of the spoon. Stir in 3oz (75gm) cheese.
6. Place 1 tablespoon sauce in each shell and sprinkle with a few breadcrumbs.
7. Place the scallop on top and cover with remaining sauce.
8. Top with crumbs and cheese and dot with small pats of butter.
9. Bake on centre shelf of oven for 20 minutes.

GRILLED SCALLOPS
Serves 4

1½lb (¾ kilo) potatoes
4 scallops
olive oil
salt and pepper
2oz (50gm) butter
a little milk
1 garlic clove
1 teaspoon chopped parsley

1. Cook potatoes.
2. Place scallops on an ovenware dish, brush with oil, sprinkle with salt and pepper and place under a medium grill.
3. Grill for 3–4 minutes on each side.
4. Cream potatoes with 1oz (25gm) butter and milk.
5. Make a border round four scallop shells then place a scallop in centre of each.
6. Heat 2 tablespoons olive oil with rest of butter and finely chopped garlic.
7. Pour over scallops and garnish with parsley.

SALMON SOUFFLE
Serves 4

2oz (50gm) butter
2oz (50gm) plain flour
½ pint (250ml) milk
1 can red salmon
1 tablespoon anchovy essence
salt and pepper
4 large eggs

1. Preheat oven to moderately hot, 400 deg F or gas 6 (200 deg C).
2. Melt the butter. Add the flour and stir over a low heat for 2–3 minutes.
3. Remove from heat and add the milk gradually, stirring all the time. Return to heat and cook, stirring, to make a smooth thick sauce.
4. Add the salmon, anchovy essence, salt and pepper. Remove from the heat.
5. Separate the eggs and add the yolks to the salmon mixture.
6. Whisk the whites until they stand in stiff peaks. Fold them into the salmon mixture, using a metal spoon.
7. Pour into a well oiled soufflé dish, or deep ovenproof dish and bake for 30 minutes.

Hot meat

As meat is expensive it is important to make the most of it and to cook it carefully. Vegetables in a casserole and a stuffing added to a roast joint make meat go much further.

GOULASH
Serves 4

1lb (½ kilo) rump or buttock steak
½oz (12gm) dripping
1lb (½ kilo) onions, thinly sliced
1 or 2 garlic cloves, chopped
1 level tablespoon paprika pepper
salt and pepper
½ level teaspoon caraway seeds
1 tablespoon tomato purée
¾ pint (375ml) beef stock
1 level tablespoon flour
4 tablespoons soured cream or yogurt

1. Wipe and trim the meat. Chop up the fat into very small pieces.
2. Put into a heavy stewpan, together with a little dripping, if necessary. Heat gently until the fat begins to melt. Discard pieces of fat.
3. Add the meat cut into small pieces and the onion and garlic.
4. Fry until the meat is browned.
5. Stir in the paprika pepper, seasoning and caraway seeds. Fry for 2–3 minutes.
6. Cover tightly and cook very gently for 40–50 minutes, stirring once or twice.
7. Add the tomato purée, stock and flour.
8. Cover and simmer gently for another hour, then taste, adding seasoning, if necessary.
9. Just before serving, stir in the soured cream or yogurt.
10. Pile a border of creamed potatoes round the edge of a serving dish, sprinkle with cheese and spoon meat and sauce in centre.

BROWN STEW
Serves 4

1–1½lb (½–¾ kilo) chuck or buttock steak
2oz (50gm) flour, seasoned with salt and pepper
1 large onion
1 large carrot
1 leek
2 sticks celery
piece of turnip
1 level teaspoon salt and pepper
1 teaspoon tomato purée
bouquet garni
¾ pint (375ml) beef stock

1. Wipe the meat and remove the fat.
2. Cut fat in small pieces and put to render down in a heavy stewpan.
3. Cut up the meat and roll it in seasoned flour.
4. Fry quickly in rendered fat, after removing shrivelled fat pieces from the pan.
5. Cut vegetables into neat, small pieces and add to the meat. Fry gently for 5 minutes.
6. Add seasoning, tomato purée, bouquet garni, then stir in stock and bring up to simmering point.
7. Cover with a lid and cook gently for 1½–2 hours.
8. Remove bouquet garni and stir in a little flour, mixed to a paste with water.
9. Cook gently for 3–4 minutes. Serve with creamed potatoes.

BEEF CASSEROLE WITH CHEESE TOPPING
Serves 4

1½lb (¾ kilo) shoulder steak
1oz (25gm) flour, seasoned with salt and pepper
2oz (50gm) dripping
2 cloves
1 garlic clove
1 bayleaf
2 tablespoons tomato purée
1½ pints (approximately ¾ litre) good stock
4 small onions, peeled
2 large carrots, cut into strips
4 small potatoes, peeled and sliced
2 tablespoons red wine
2oz (50gm) Cheddar cheese

1. Preheat oven to cool, 300 deg F or gas 2 (150 deg C).
2. Cut steak into 1-inch cubes.
3. Toss in seasoned flour and brown in the dripping.
4. Add crushed cloves, garlic, bayleaf, tomato purée, stock, onions, carrots, potatoes and red wine.
5. Place in an ovenware casserole dish.
6. Cover and cook in centre of oven for 1½ hours.
7. Remove and grate cheese over top of casserole.
8. Increase oven setting to hot, 425 deg F or gas 7 (220 deg C).
9. Return casserole, uncovered, to oven and cook until cheese is crisp and golden.

CURRIED BEEF
Serves 4

1lb (½ kilo) buttock steak
2oz (50gm) flour, seasoned with
salt and pepper
8oz (200gm) onions
1 level teaspoon salt
1 level teaspoon pepper
¾ pint (375ml) beef stock
1 can (1 pint or approximately
½ litre) curry sauce
1 teaspoon chopped parsley

1. Wipe the meat, remove the fat
and cut into tiny pieces.
2. Fry gently in a heavy stewpan
until the fat has melted. (Discard
any shrivelled fat tissue.) If meat
is lean, use ½oz (12gm) dripping
instead of the above process.
3. Cut up the lean meat and roll it
in seasoned flour.
4. Fry quickly in hot fat until
browned.
5. Add the thinly sliced onions
and seasoning.
6. Cover tightly and cook gently
for 4–5 minutes.
7. Add stock and cover with
greased paper and a lid. Cook
until the meat is tender and the
liquid absorbed.
8. Stir the curry sauce into the
meat and simmer gently for 10–15
minutes.
9. Dish up in a border of boiled
rice.

CHEESE-TOPPED STEAKS
Serves 4

4 fillet or rump steaks
2oz (50gm) butter
salt and pepper
4oz (100gm) Lancashire cheese,
crumbled
watercress
4 tomatoes

1. Beat the steaks with the handle
of a heavy knife.
2. Melt the butter and brush over
the steaks. Season.
3. Cook under a very hot grill.
4. Turn the steaks over and
season again.
5. Scatter the cheese over and
continue to cook until browned
and cooked through.
6. Serve garnished with
watercress and grilled tomatoes.

AUSTRIAN BEEF OLIVES
(Illustrated on page 53)
Serves 4

1oz (25gm) butter
1 small onion, chopped
2 tablespoons fresh, white
breadcrumbs
2oz (50gm) mushrooms, diced
2 teaspoons freshly chopped
parsley
pinch of mixed herbs
salt and pepper
1 small egg, well beaten
4 slices rump steak about 2lb (1
kilo)
1oz (25gm) flour, seasoned with
salt and pepper
1oz (25gm) butter
2 tablespoons oil
2 tablespoons tomato purée
½ pint (250ml) beef stock
1 bayleaf
2 cartons natural yogurt
1 onion, sliced
1 tomato, sliced
½ cucumber, sliced
chopped chives

1. Preheat oven to moderate, 350
deg F or gas 4 (180 deg C).
2. Combine together butter,
onion, breadcrumbs, mushrooms,
herbs and seasoning. Bind with
egg.
3. Spread over the steaks, roll up
and secure with string or wooden
cocktail sticks. Roll in flour.
4. Melt butter with oil in pan.
Brown the meat on all sides, then
gradually add tomato purée, stock
and bayleaf. Cover.
5. Simmer gently for 30 minutes
then transfer to a casserole and
place in centre of oven for
1½ hours.
6. Remove meat from casserole to
serving dish.
7. Stir yogurt into liquor, then
reheat without boiling.
8. Pour sauce over meat and serve
with a salad of sliced onion,
tomato and cucumber garnished
with chopped chives.

ORANGE STEAKS
(Illustrated on page 54)
Serves 4

4 medium-sized steaks
8 small mushrooms, sliced
2oz (50gm) butter
1oz (25gm) blanched almonds
3oz (75gm) seedless raisins
3 tablespoons white
breadcrumbs
2 oranges
potato chips and parsley to
garnish

1. Grill the steaks and arrange
them in an ovenware dish.
2. Fry the mushrooms in half the
butter and place them on top of
the steaks.
3. Lightly chop the nuts and
raisins together and mix with the
crumbs and juice of 1 orange.
4. Place mixture on top of the
mushrooms.
5. Put the dish under a hot grill
for a few moments with the rest of
the butter to lightly brown.
Garnish with twists of sliced
orange, potato chips and parsley.

FAMILY CORNISH PASTY
Serves 4

8oz (200gm) rump steak
1 large onion
8oz (200gm) raw potato
salt and pepper
a little stock
shortcrust pastry made with
6oz (150gm) flour (see Basic
recipes, page 100)
1 egg, beaten

1. Preheat oven to moderate, 350
deg F or gas 4 (180 deg C).
2. Trim steak and cut into small,
neat pieces.
3. Mix with the chopped onion,
diced potato, seasoning and stock.
4. Roll out the pastry into a
round the size of a large dinner
plate and put the filling on to one
half.
5. Damp the edges and fold pastry
over to form a half-moon shape.
Seal the edges securely and make
parallel slits in the top.
6. Glaze with egg and bake in
centre of oven for 1 hour.
7. Test the meat with a knife to
see if it is tender before removing
pasties from oven.

SWISS STEAK
Serves 4

1 medium onion, sliced
1oz (25gm) dripping
1 piece (1½lb or ¾ kilo) chuck
steak, cut ¾-inch thick
1 packet (1 pint or
approximately ½ litre) tomato
soup
½ pint (250ml) cold water
1 teaspoon malt vinegar

1. Preheat oven to cool, 300 deg F
or gas 2 (150 deg C).
2. Fry the onions in the dripping
in a frying pan until golden
brown.
3. Transfer to a large, shallow
casserole.
4. Trim the meat. Coat with half
the dry contents of the packet of
tomato soup.
5. Fry lightly on both sides in the
remainder of the fat in the frying
pan until browned. Place in the
casserole.
6. Remove the frying pan from
the heat and add the remainder of
the soup mix.
7. Add the water and vinegar and
stir until smooth. Bring to the
boil, stirring all the time, then
pour over the meat and onions.
8. Cover with a lid and cook in
centre of oven for 1½–2 hours until
the steak is tender.
9. Serve with creamy mashed
potato.

STUFFED BEEF ROLLS
Serves 4

1oz (25gm) suet
2oz (50gm) fresh breadcrumbs
1 tablespoon chopped parsley
good sprinkle mixed, dried
herbs
salt and pepper
1 egg, separated
1lb (½ kilo) chuck steak, cut
into 4 even-sized pieces
1oz (25gm) dripping
1oz (25gm) flour
1 pint (approximately ¾ litre)
stock

1. Preheat oven to moderate, 350
deg F or gas 4 (180 deg C).
2. Mix suet, breadcrumbs and
parsley with herbs and seasoning.
Bind with beaten egg yolk.
3. Beat pieces of steak with a
rolling pin. Spread stuffing on
each piece of steak and roll up.
4. Tie securely and fry rolls in
dripping until brown.
5. Remove meat. Add flour and
leave to brown, then blend in the
stock.
6. Replace meat, cover and bake
for 1½ hours in centre of oven.

BEAN AND BEEF STEW
Serves 4

1oz (25gm) lard
6oz (150gm) onion, finely sliced
1½lb (¾ kilo) chuck steak, cut
into 1½-inch cubes
½oz (12gm) flour, seasoned with
salt and pepper
1 can (15½oz or approximately ½
kilo) butter beans
½ pint (250ml) beef stock
2 tablespoons red wine
(optional)
1 red pepper, finely shredded

1. Melt the lard in a saucepan.
Add the onion and fry gently for
5 minutes until tender and just
golden. Remove from pan.
2. Coat the steak with seasoned
flour.
3. Fry meat in the remaining fat
until browned on all sides and
return onions to pan.
4. Drain the butter beans and add
the liquor to the meat with the
stock and wine, if used.
5. Bring to the boil, cover the pan
and simmer very slowly for 1½–2
hours until the meat is tender.
6. Add the red pepper and adjust
seasoning if necessary.
7. Add the butter beans and
continue cooking the stew for a
further 5 minutes over a low heat.

BEEF AND TOMATO HOT POT
Serves 4

1lb (½ kilo) stewing steak
1oz (25gm) flour seasoned with
salt and pepper
1lb (½ kilo) tomatoes, skinned
and sliced
2 tablespoons water

1. Preheat oven to very moderate,
325 deg F or gas 3 (170 deg C).
2. Trim the steak and cut up into
narrow strips.
3. Toss the meat in seasoned
flour.
4. Layer meat and tomatoes in a
casserole.
5. Add the water and cover with a
very well fitting lid.
6. Place below the centre shelf of
oven and simmer for 2½ hours.
Serve with mashed potato.

BEEF AND CREAM CASSEROLE
Serves 4

2lb (1 kilo) stewing steak
2oz (50gm) flour, seasoned with salt and pepper
2oz (50gm) dripping
½ pint (250ml) tomato juice or water
1 small onion, finely chopped
½ teaspoon dried, mixed herbs
4oz (100gm) peas
¼ pint (125ml) soured or fresh cream
1 tablespoon horseradish sauce

1. Cut the meat into 1-inch cubes and coat with flour.
2. Heat the dripping in a frying pan, add the meat and brown quickly.
3. Add the tomato juice or water, onion and herbs.
4. Turn into a saucepan, cover and simmer for 2¼ hours.
5. Add the peas and cook for a further 10 minutes.
6. Stir in cream and horseradish sauce just before serving.

BEEF IN BEER
Serves 4

1lb (½ kilo) stewing steak, skirt or chuck
1oz (25gm) flour
1oz (25gm) butter
2 large onions, sliced
salt and pepper
1 teaspoon brown sugar
grated nutmeg
1 garlic clove
1 bayleaf
¼ pint (125ml) beef stock
½ pint (250ml) stout

1. Preheat oven to cool, 275 deg F or gas 1 (140 deg C).
2. Cut the meat into 2-inch pieces and toss in flour.
3. Melt the butter in a saucepan or casserole and add onions.
4. Add the meat and brown on all sides.
5. Season the meat and onions, then add sugar, nutmeg, crushed garlic and bayleaf.
6. Add stock and stout to the meat.
7. Simmer the meat in a casserole with a well-fitting lid for 2½–3 hours.
8. Serve with carrots and noodles.

POTTED BEEF STEAK
Serves 4

6oz (150gm) streaky bacon
1lb (½ kilo) stewing steak
salt and pepper
1 teaspoon mixed herbs
½ teaspoon grated nutmeg
¼ pint (125ml) stock

1. Preheat oven to very moderate, 325 deg F or gas 3 (170 deg C).
2. Discard bacon rinds and chop up bacon.
3. Dice up the steak.
4. Layer the bacon and steak in a pie dish, sprinkling each layer with salt, pepper, herbs and nutmeg.
5. Pour stock over and cover tightly. Bake in a tin of cold water in centre of oven for 2 hours.
6. Press under a weight, then, when cold, turn out, slice and serve with salad.

BRAISED BEEF
Serves 6

2lb (1 kilo) joint topside of beef
fat for frying
1 onion, sliced
2 sticks celery, sliced
1 turnip, diced
4 carrots, sliced
bouquet garni
bacon rinds
¾ pint (375ml) beef stock
sliced carrots, turnips and peas to garnish

1. Preheat oven to moderate, 350 deg F or gas 4 (180 deg C).
2. Prepare joint as for roasting.
3. Melt fat in a braising pan or large saucepan and brown the meat on all sides.
4. Lift meat out and lightly fry the prepared vegetables in the pan. Return meat to pan.
5. Add bouquet garni, bacon rinds and enough stock to cover vegetables.
6. Cook in centre of oven for 1–1½ hours.
7. Increase oven temperature to moderately hot, 400 deg F or gas 6 (200 deg C), remove lid from pan and cook for a further 15 minutes.
8. Garnish with freshly cooked, sliced vegetables and peas.

CRUSTY BEEF MINCE
Serves 4

1oz (25gm) dripping
2 onions, sliced
1½lb (¾ kilo) lean minced beef
½ pint (250ml) rich brown gravy
1 tablespoon tomato pulp
1 bayleaf
pinch of thyme
salt and pepper
1 Vienna loaf
1 garlic clove
2–3oz (50–75gm) butter

1. Preheat oven to moderate to moderately hot, 375 deg F or gas 5 (190 deg C).
2. Heat the dripping in a pan and lightly fry the onion until tender but not browned.
3. Add the meat and stir for a few moments then add the gravy, tomato pulp, herbs and seasoning.
4. Simmer for 5 minutes.
5. Turn into a fireproof dish. Cover and cook in the centre of oven for 15 minutes.
6. Remove bayleaf.
7. Slice the bread.
8. Crush the garlic and blend with the butter and a little salt.
9. Spread the garlic butter on the bread and arrange on the top of the dish.
10. Return to oven to brown.

BEEF PIZZA
Serves 4

8oz (200gm) self-raising flour
3oz (75gm) margarine
pinch of mixed herbs
salt and pepper
milk to mix
1 medium can minced beef with
onions
2 slices processed cheese, cut
into strips
1 tomato

1. Preheat oven to hot, 425 deg F
or gas 7 (220 deg C).
2. Sift flour into a bowl. Rub in
margarine until mixture resembles
fine breadcrumbs.
3. Add herbs and seasoning.
4. Mix to a soft dough with milk,
then roll out into a 10-inch round,
using a dinner plate as a guide.
Place on a baking sheet.
5. Spread minced beef with onions
over the dough.
6. Arrange strips of cheese on top
like the spokes of a wheel.
7. Slice the tomato and place a
slice in between each strip of
cheese.
8. Bake in centre of oven for 20
minutes. Serve hot.

GOLDEN FRITTERS
Serves 4

1 large potato, peeled and
grated
8oz (200gm) minced beef
1 medium onion, chopped
1 teaspoon Worcestershire
sauce
1 dessertspoon chopped
parsley
pinch of mixed herbs
salt and pepper
4oz (100gm) plain flour
pinch of salt
1 egg
¼ pint (125ml) milk
deep fat for frying

1. Mix potato with beef, onion
and sauce.
2. Stir in parsley, herbs and
seasoning.
3. Form into small rounds.
4. Sift flour into a bowl. Add salt
and break egg into the centre,
then gradually beat in milk.
5. Coat each piece of meat in this
batter and fry until crisp and
golden in deep hot fat. Drain.
6. Serve with a green salad.

MINCED BEEF COBBLERS
Serves 4

12oz (300gm) minced beef
salt and pepper
½ pint (250ml) stock
2 teaspoons tomato pulp
1 small onion, chopped
8oz (200gm) plain flour
1 level teaspoon baking powder
1 teaspoon mixed herbs
2oz (50gm) lard
milk to mix

1. Preheat oven to hot, 425 deg F
or gas 7 (220 deg C).
2. Put minced beef into a pan
with the salt and pepper.
3. Add stock, tomato pulp and
onion.
4. Simmer until the minced beef is
cooked through.
5. Divide into four individual
dishes.
6. Sift the flour and baking
powder into a bowl. Season and
add herbs.
7. Rub in the lard till mixture
resembles fine breadcrumbs. Mix
in enough milk to make a dough.
8. Knead lightly and cut into
rounds.
9. Put two or three rounds on top
of each dish.
10. Bake in centre of oven for
about 15 minutes, until the dough
rounds have risen and browned.

BEEF ROLY POLY
Serves 4

suet crust pastry made with
8oz (200gm) flour (see Basic
recipes, page 100)
8oz (200gm) lean raw beef,
minced
1 level teaspoon chopped
parsley
1 small onion, chopped
large pinch of mixed herbs
3 tablespoons gravy
salt and pepper

1. Roll out pastry to an oblong,
approximately 10–12 inches long.
2. Mix rest of ingredients
together and spread over pastry
to within 1 inch of the edges.
3. Moisten edges with cold water,
then roll up starting from one of
the shorter sides.
4. Wrap in aluminium foil or
greaseproof paper and steam for 2
hours.
5. Serve hot with a rich brown
gravy.

BEEFBURGERS
Serves 6

1lb (½ kilo) minced beef
salt and pepper
4oz (100gm) white breadcrumbs
1 onion, finely chopped
olive oil
6 soft rolls

1. Mix the minced beef, seasoning,
breadcrumbs and onion together.
2. Divide mixture into six
portions.
3. Brush with olive oil and grill
on both sides.
4. When cooked, sandwich each
beefburger in a hot, soft roll.
Serve hot with plenty of mustard.

BEEF RICE PEASANT STYLE
Serves 4

1 large onion, chopped
1 garlic clove, chopped
cooking oil
4 medium carrots
1lb (½ kilo) minced beef
1 small can tomatoes
1 tablespoon tomato purée
1 bayleaf
salt and pepper
8oz (200gm) long-grain rice
1 pint water
1 teaspoon salt

1. Fry onion and garlic in oil until tender.
2. Add chopped carrot, minced beef and fry until brown.
3. Add tomatoes and tomato purée, bayleaf and seasoning. Simmer until cooked.
4. Put rice, water and salt into a large saucepan.
5. Bring to the boil and stir once. Lower heat to simmer.
6. Cover pan and cook for about 15 minutes, without removing lid or stirring.
7. Fork out on to a serving dish and arrange beef in the centre.

FRICADELLES
Serves 3–4

1 slice bread, ½ inch thick
2 tablespoons milk
6oz (150gm) minced beef
1 small onion, finely chopped
pinch of mixed herbs
salt and pepper
1 egg, beaten
breadcrumbs for coating
6oz (150gm) fat for frying

1. Remove crusts, then soak bread in milk.
2. Squeeze bread and mix with meat, onion, herbs, seasoning and a little egg.
3. Divide mixture into about 12 portions and roll into small balls.
4. Coat with rest of egg and breadcrumbs, then fry for 10 minutes in hot fat. Drain.
5. Serve with a tomato sauce.

HAMBURGERS WITH MUSHROOM SAUCE
Serves 4

1lb (½ kilo) minced beef
1 small onion, minced
1 teaspoon salt
¼ teaspoon pepper
1 can condensed cream of mushroom soup
1oz (25gm) butter
¼ pint (125ml) milk
a few cooked mushrooms
a little grated cheese or a pinch of curry powder

1. Mix minced beef, onion, salt and pepper together without handling too much.
2. Shape gently into four hamburgers and grill for 8–12 minutes, or fry in a little fat for 4–8 minutes, turning them over once.
3. Combine rest of ingredients together in a pan and heat gently. Pour sauce over hamburgers and serve at once.

BEEF RECHAUFFE WITH CREAMED POTATO
Serves 4

12oz (300gm) cooked beef
2 bacon rashers
2 small onions
salt and pepper
1 tablespoon chopped parsley
¼ pint (125ml) stock or gravy
1 tablespoon vinegar
creamed potato

1. Preheat oven to moderately hot, 400 deg F or gas 6 (200 deg C).
2. Cut beef into wafer-thin slices and put a few of them into a greased baking dish.
3. Dice the bacon and fry it with the sliced onions.
4. When browned, add salt, pepper and parsley.
5. Put alternate layers of this mixture and cold beef into the baking dish.
6. Heat stock or gravy, add vinegar and pour into the dish.
7. Cover and bake in centre of oven for 15 minutes. Take off the cover, spoon some well-seasoned, hot, creamed potato over and serve at once.

WINTER BRAISE
Serves 4

1oz (25gm) dripping
1 onion, chopped
1 carrot, chopped
1 streaky bacon rasher, chopped
1½lb (¾ kilo) topside of beef
½ teaspoon tomato purée
1oz (25gm) flour
1 pint (approximately ½ litre) brown stock

1. Melt the dripping in a heavy pan.
2. Fry the onion, carrot and bacon.
3. Cut meat into 2-inch squares. Add to the vegetables and brown.
4. Remove meat and keep hot.
5. Mix tomato purée into pan.
6. Add flour and cook until brown. Beat in stock.
7. Replace meat and simmer for 2 hours, until meat is tender.
8. Serve with potatoes and a green vegetable.

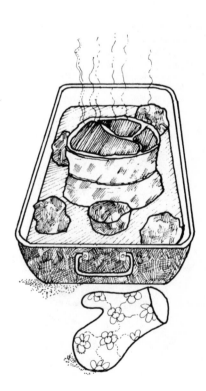

PEPPERED LAMB CASSEROLE
Serves 6

2¼–3lb (approximately 1½ kilo) shoulder of lamb
1 teaspoon salt
½ teaspoon black pepper
good pinch of cayenne pepper
1 teaspoon ground mace
4 tablespoons oil
1 onion, chopped
2 garlic cloves, crushed
¼ pint (125ml) red wine
3 peppers, shredded (red and and green mixed)
1½lb (¾ kilo) tomatoes, skinned and sliced
1 level tablespoon chopped parsley

1. Preheat oven to moderate, 350 deg F or gas 4 (180 deg C).
2. Bone the lamb and cut meat into 2-inch squares, removing any excess fat.
3. Turn into a bowl and sprinkle with half the salt, pepper, cayenne and mace.
4. Leave for 30 minutes, then turn meat over and sprinkle with rest of seasoning.
5. Fry meat in oil until golden.
6. Add onion and garlic and cook until tender.
7. Heat wine in a separate pan, then pour over meat. Turn into a casserole.
8. Blanch peppers in boiling water for 2 minutes and add to casserole.
9. Cook below the centre of oven for 1½ hours.
10. Add tomatoes 20 minutes before the end of cooking time.
11. Sprinkle with parsley.

ORIENTAL LAMB
(Illustrated on page 53)
Serves 4

2oz (50gm) dried apricots, soaked
2oz (50gm) breadcrumbs
2oz (50gm) ham, chopped
1 egg, beaten
salt and pepper
1 shoulder of lamb or best end neck of lamb, boned
2oz (50gm) fat
8oz (200gm) long-grain rice
2 onions, chopped
1 dessertspoon curry powder
1 pint (approximately ½ litre) beef stock
slices red and green pepper to garnish

1. Preheat oven to moderate, 350 deg F or gas 4 (180 deg C).
2. Combine chopped apricots, breadcrumbs, ham, egg and seasoning to make stuffing.
3. Spread on the meat, roll up and tie firmly.
4. Melt the fat and brown meat on all sides.
5. Remove and gently fry rice, onion and curry powder.
6. Add meat and pour stock over.
7. Cover and cook in centre of oven for 2–2½ hours, adding more stock, if necessary.
8. Garnish with slices of red and green pepper.

RISOTTO-STUFFED SHOULDER OF LAMB
Serves 4–6

1oz (25gm) dripping
1 large onion, chopped
4oz (100gm) long-grain rice
½ pint (250ml) stock
2 large tomatoes, skinned and diced
salt and pepper
3lb (1½ kilo) shoulder of lamb, boned

1. Preheat oven to moderate, 350 deg F or gas 4 (180 deg C).
2. Melt dripping in a saucepan and fry onion until tender.
3. Add rice and cook until it changes colour.
4. Add stock, bring to the boil and stir once.
5. Lower heat. Cover tightly and simmer for about 15 minutes.
6. Add tomatoes and seasoning. Cook a few minutes longer then cool.
7. Lay shoulder of lamb, skin side down, on a flat surface. Spread with risotto.
8. Roll up and secure with string. Place in a roasting pan and cook for 1½–1¾ hours on centre shelf. Baste at intervals during cooking.

FRUITED VICTORIAN LAMB
Serves 4

8oz (200gm) plums
3oz (75gm) fresh, white breadcrumbs
¼ level teaspoon mixed spice
salt and pepper
1 tablespoon lemon juice
1oz (25gm) butter, melted
1 egg, beaten
1 4-bone loin of lamb, boned

1. Preheat oven to hot, 425 deg F or gas 7 (220 deg C).
2. Skin, stone and roughly chop the plums.
3. Mix with the remaining ingredients.
4. Spread down centre of meat, roll up and tie securely with string.
5. Roast in centre of oven, allowing 20 minutes to the pound (½ kilo) and 25 minutes over.

Lancashire hot pot (see page 55)

Pineapple pork chops with potatoes and salad (see page 58)

Austrian beef olives with a side salad (see page 47)

Oriental lamb (see page 52)

Orange steaks (see page 47)   Orange-sauced duck with orange salad (see page 81)

Turkey pancakes (see page 83)   Crispy chicken joints with potatoes and peas (see page 69)

LANCASHIRE HOT POT
(Illustrated on page 53)
Serves 3–4

1½lb (¾ kilo) middle neck of
mutton or lamb
2 level teaspoons salt
1½lb (¾ kilo) potatoes
2 onions
1 carrot
3 sticks celery
½ pint (250ml) beef stock

1. Preheat oven to moderate, 350
deg F or gas 4 (180 deg C).
2. Wipe and trim the meat of
excess fat. Divide into joints or
cut into pieces and sprinkle with
salt.
3. Prepare the vegetables, slice
the potatoes and cut remaining
vegetables into pieces.
4. Arrange the meat and
vegetables in layers in a casserole,
reserving the potatoes for the top.
5. Add the stock and top with a
layer of neatly arranged potatoes.
6. Cover with greaseproof paper
and a lid and bake in centre of
oven for 1½ hours. Remove the lid
and paper.
7. Replace in the oven for a
further 30 minutes to brown the
top.

LAMB AND LEEK STEW
Serves 4

1½lb (¾ kilo) middle neck of
lamb
1oz (25gm) dripping
2 pints (approximately 1 litre)
stock
salt and pepper
1lb (½ kilo) potatoes, sliced
2 leeks, sliced
3 tomatoes, skinned

1. Cut the lamb into pieces.
2. Cook in the dripping in a
saucepan until beginning to
brown.
3. Add the stock and season.
4. Cover and cook gently for 30
minutes.
5. Skim off any fat.
6. Add potatoes, leeks and
tomatoes and simmer for a further
30 minutes.

HARICOT OF MUTTON
Serves 4

1½lb (¾ kilo) neck of mutton
1oz (25gm) dripping
¾ pint (375ml) stock
bunch of mixed herbs
salt and pepper
3oz (75gm) haricot beans,
soaked
8oz (200gm) carrots
1 turnip
1 tablespoon flour

1. Trim the meat, cutting off
excess fat and dividing into
chops.
2. Melt the dripping and fry
chops on all sides.
3. Drain off the fat and add the
stock, herbs, seasoning, beans,
carrots and turnip to the pan.
4. Cover and simmer slowly for 1½
hours.
5. Put the meat on a serving dish,
removing the herbs. Thicken the
gravy with flour, blended with
cold water.
6. Cook for several minutes, then
pour the gravy over the meat and
serve at once.

IRISH PIE
Serves 4

1½lb (¾ kilo) scrag of middle
neck of lamb
2 teaspoons salt
½ teaspoon pepper
2lb (1 kilo) cooking apples
1lb (½ kilo) onions, sliced
½ pint (250ml) boiling water
suet crust pastry made with
6oz (150gm) flour (see Basic
recipes, page 100)

1. Preheat oven to moderate to
moderately hot, 375 deg F
or gas 5 (190 deg C).
2. Cut the meat into bite-sized
pieces and put into the bottom of
a deep pie dish.
3. Sprinkle with salt and pepper.
4. Peel and slice the apples and
arrange them in alternate layers
with onion on the meat. Pour
boiling water over.
5. Make the pastry, roll it out and
cover pie dish.
6. Bake on second shelf from top
of oven for 1½ hours.
7. Serve with diced carrots, peas
and mashed potatoes.

COUNTRY LAMB CHOPS
Serves 4

4 lamb chops
2oz (50gm) butter
1lb (½ kilo) potatoes, peeled and
sliced
4 onions, skinned and sliced
salt and pepper
4 cooking apples
¾oz (18gm) flour
½ pint (250ml) stock
¼ pint (125ml) cider

1. Preheat oven to moderate, 350
deg F or gas 4 (180 deg C).
2. Trim the fat off the chops and
brown quickly in butter in a pan.
3. Remove and keep hot.
4. Fry potatoes and onions.
5. Put half the potatoes and
onions in an ovenware dish.
6. Top with the chops, then add
rest of potatoes and onions and
season very well.
7. Peel and core apples, then slice
them; place over the top of the
dish.
8. Stir flour into the pan and cook
until just golden brown.
9. Mix in stock and cider and stir
until thickened.
10. Strain over meat and
vegetables and cook in centre of
oven for 1 hour.

REDCURRANT LAMB
Serves 6

3lb (1½ kilo) leg of lamb
2 rounded tablespoons
redcurrant jelly
2 tablespoons vinegar
1 small onion, chopped
4 tomatoes, sliced

1. Preheat oven to hot, 425 deg F
or gas 7 (220 deg C).
2. Put the lamb on a large piece
of foil and spread redcurrant jelly
over it.
3. Pour vinegar over and sprinkle
with onion.
4. Wrap in the foil, then bake in
centre of oven, allowing 35
minutes per pound (½ kilo).
5. Unwrap the foil for the last 20
minutes and surround the lamb
with tomatoes.
6. Serve with new potatoes and
young carrots.

FRYING PAN SCRAMBLE
Serves 4

4 lamb chops
1oz (25gm) lard
1 medium onion, sliced
4 potatoes
1 carrot, grated
¼ pint (125ml) water or stock
salt and pepper
2 tomatoes, sliced
4oz (100gm) cabbage, chopped

1. Trim the excess fat off the
chops and melt the lard in the
pan.
2. Fry chops on both sides.
3. Add onion and cook until
tender.
4. Peel the potatoes and slice
thinly.
5. Add to the pan with the carrot.
6. Add water or stock, season and
simmer for 20 minutes.
7. Add tomatoes and cabbage and
cook for a further 15 minutes.

LAMB CUTLETS PASCALE
Serves 4

3 onions
2 tablespoons corn oil
2oz (50gm) long-grain rice
¼ pint (125ml) stock
8 lamb cutlets
2 packets (½ pint or 250ml each)
white sauce mix
¾ pint (375ml) milk
6oz (150gm) cheese, grated
1 egg yolk
1 packet frozen peas, cooked

1. Chop the onions and fry in 1
tablespoon oil.
2. Stir in the rice.
3. Add the stock, cover with
greaseproof paper and a lid and
cook gently for 20–30 minutes.
4. Trim the cutlets and fry in rest
of oil for 10 minutes.
5. Remove and drain.
6. Place on a serving dish and pile
the onion mixture on top.
7. Place the sauce mix in a pan
and blend with the milk.
8. Bring to the boil, stirring all
the time. Boil for one minute.
9. Stir in the grated cheese and
egg yolk and pour over cutlets to
serve.

LAMB CUTLETS AND FRIED CUCUMBER
Serves 4

4 lamb cutlets
salt and pepper
1 egg
2oz (50gm) breadcrumbs
4oz (100gm) lard
½ cucumber
1lb (½ kilo) fresh or canned,
cooked new potatoes

1. Trim the cutlets and sprinkle
with seasoning.
2. Dip in beaten egg and coat
with breadcrumbs.
3. Fry on both sides in half the
lard until cooked through and
golden brown. Keep hot.
4. Peel and dice the cucumber and
discard the seeds.
5. Season the cucumber and melt
the rest of the lard in a pan.
6. Cook the cucumber for about
10 minutes in the pan until really
tender.
7. Spoon the hot new potatoes on
to either end of a hot dish.
8. Arrange the cutlets in the dish
and put the cucumber in the
centre.

CHEESED LAMB CHOPS
Serves 4

Lamb chops hidden under a crispy
topping of potatoes.

4 lamb chops
2oz (50gm) butter
12oz (300gm) potatoes, sliced
1 onion, minced
salt and pepper
½ pint (250ml) stock
1 tomato
3oz (75gm) Cheddar cheese,
grated
1. Preheat oven to moderate, 350
deg F or gas 4 (180 deg C).
2. Trim chops, then brown
quickly in hot butter.
3. Put in a casserole dish and top
with potatoes and onion.
4. Season and pour on stock.
5. Slice the tomato, place over the
potatoes and sprinkle with grated
cheese.
6. Cover and cook in centre of
oven for 1½ hours. Remove cover
to allow top to brown before
serving.

LAMB CASSEROLE
Serves 4

4 lamb chops
½oz (12gm) fresh mint, chopped
8oz (200gm) tomatoes, skinned
2 onions, sliced
½ cucumber, sliced
salt and pepper
1 dessertspoon brown sugar
3 tablespoons vinegar
4oz (100gm) fresh breadcrumbs
2oz (50gm) Cheddar cheese, grated

1. Preheat oven to moderate, 350 deg F or gas 4 (180 deg C).
2. Place chops on bottom of casserole dish.
3. Sprinkle with mint and layer tomatoes, onions and cucumber alternatively on top, seasoning well between each layer.
4. Add sugar and vinegar and sprinkle breadcrumbs and cheese on top.
5. Cook in centre of oven for 1½ hours.

SOUTHDOWN LAMB PIE
Serves 4

2 medium onions, chopped
1oz (25gm) lard
2lb (1 kilo) breast of lamb, boned
½oz (12gm) flour
½ pint (250ml) stock
salt and pepper
1 level teaspoon dill
2oz (50gm) cheese, grated
shortcrust pastry made with 4oz (100gm) flour (see Basic recipes, page 100)

1. Preheat oven to moderately hot, 400 deg F or gas 6 (200 deg C).
2. Fry onions lightly in lard.
3. Cut lamb into small pieces. Add to pan with the onions, and fry until brown.
4. Add flour and cook a little.
5. Stir in stock and seasoning.
6. Simmer for about 1 hour until meat is tender and liquid absorbed.
7. Place lamb in a pie dish. Mix in dill and cheese. Allow to cool.
8. Cover with pastry and bake in centre of oven for 25–30 minutes until nicely browned.
9. Serve hot with vegetables.

LAMB RISSOLES
Makes 8 rissoles

1lb (½ kilo) cooked lamb, minced
3oz (75gm) cornflakes, crushed
½ level teaspoon mixed herbs
salt and pepper
2 level tablespoons tomato ketchup
1 teaspoon Worcestershire sauce
3 eggs
oil or cooking fat for frying

1. Mix together lamb, 2oz (50gm) cornflakes, herbs and seasoning.
2. Bind together with ketchup, Worcestershire sauce and 2 beaten eggs.
3. Shape into eight rissoles.
4. Coat each rissole in beaten egg and then in rest of cornflake crumbs.
5. Fry gently in shallow fat for about 3 minutes on each side.
6. Drain and serve hot or cold.

BARBECUED LAMB SLICES
Serves 4

12oz (300gm) cold lamb
1½oz (37gm) butter, melted
3 teaspoons vinegar
4 tablespoons redcurrant jelly
¼ pint (125ml) stock
a little dry mustard
salt and pepper

1. Cut the lamb into neat slices.
2. Make a piquant sauce by melting the butter in a frying pan, adding vinegar, redcurrant jelly, stock and seasonings.
3. Add the slices of meat and turn them in the sauce until they are well covered and heated through.
4. Serve on a hot dish, pour over the remaining sauce and serve at once.

CHEESE-TOPPED LAMB
Serves 4

1oz (25gm) butter
1 large onion, minced
2 sprigs of parsley, chopped
2 bacon rashers, minced
12oz (300gm) cooked lamb, minced
½ pint (250ml) gravy
¼ pint (125ml) tomato juice
3 tomatoes, skinned
salt and pepper
¼ pint (125ml) double cream
1oz (25gm) Cheddar cheese, grated

1. Melt the butter in a pan and add the onion. Cook until tender.
2. Add parsley, bacon, lamb, gravy and tomato juice and allow to heat through gently.
3. Chop and add the tomatoes and seasoning.
4. Cover the pan and allow to simmer slowly for 1 hour.
5. Turn into a casserole dish. Pour the cream over and sprinkle with cheese. Brown under a very hot grill.

PINEAPPLE PORK CHOPS
(Illustrated on page 53)
Serves 4

2oz (50gm) lard or a little oil
4 thick pork chops
1 garlic clove
1 medium can pineapple rings
¾oz (18gm) cornflour
1 tablespoon tomato purée
1 bayleaf
1 stick celery, chopped
1 sprig of parsley
1 sprig of thyme
salt and pepper
1 small onion, chopped

1. Preheat oven to moderate, 350 deg F or gas 4 (180 deg C).
2. Melt the lard or oil in a pan. Fry the pork chops until brown on each side but not cooked through.
3. Put into a casserole which has been rubbed round with a clove of garlic.
4. Top each chop with a pineapple ring and reserve the juice.
5. Blend the pineapple juice with the cornflour and tomato purée.
6. Add bayleaf, celery, parsley and thyme.
7. Season very well and add the onion.
8. Pour over the pork and cover the casserole with a well fitting lid.
9. Put in centre of oven for 1½ hours. Take off the lid for the last 20 minutes.
10. Serve with new potatoes garnished with chopped parsley, and a green salad.

PORK CHOPS AND SUGARED APPLES
Serves 4

fat for frying
4 loin pork chops
2 tablespoons minced onion
3 tomatoes, chopped and sieved
salt and pepper
2 teaspoons grated orange rind
¼ pint (125ml) orange juice
4oz (100gm) granulated sugar
4 firm red apples

1. Heat a little fat in a thick pan, add the meat and brown it on both sides.
2. Add the onion, tomato and seasoning, then cover.
3. Simmer for 30 minutes, or until meat is tender.
4. Heat orange rind, juice and sugar in a pan until the sugar dissolves.
5. Wipe and quarter the apples. Do not peel, but remove the cores and cook carefully in the orange syrup until soft but unbroken.
6. Serve pork surrounded with the apples.

SPARE RIB CHOPS WITH ALMONDS
Serves 4

1 tablespoon dry mustard
1 tablespoon brown sugar
4 pork spare rib chops
1oz (25gm) almonds, shredded
salt and pepper

1. Mix the mustard and sugar together and sprinkle over the chops. Grill until tender.
2. Sprinkle almonds over the pork and season.
3. Return under grill to brown the almonds. Serve with fried potatoes and a vegetable.

BRAISED PORK CHOPS
Serves 4

4 loin pork chops
3oz (75gm) butter
1 large onion, chopped
1 teaspoon flour
1 level teaspoon salt
2 level teaspoons made mustard
pepper
1 pint (approximately ½ litre) chicken stock
1 tablespoon chopped pickle

1. Bone the meat with a sharp knife.
2. Cut each chop in half horizontally, but do not split chops entirely through. Open each out to a butterfly shape.
3. Heat half the butter in a frying pan and brown the chops on both sides. Remove and keep hot.
4. Add rest of butter to the pan and cook the onion until tender.
5. Mix in the flour, salt, mustard and shake of pepper.
6. Heat the stock and add to the pan with the pickle. Simmer for 5 minutes.
7. Add chops to the pan and cook for a further 14 minutes. Serve hot.

PORK AND APPLE CASSEROLE
Serves 4

1lb (½ kilo) pork
salt and pepper
1 cooking apple
1 onion, chopped
¼ pint (125ml) stock
4 tablespoons breadcrumbs
1oz (25gm) suet
1 dessertspoon chopped parsley

1. Preheat oven to moderate to moderately hot, 375 deg F or gas 5 (190 deg C).
2. Cut the pork into thin slices. Put half into the bottom of a casserole.
3. Season well and cover with the slices of apple.
4. Sprinkle with onion.
5. Add rest of pork and the stock.
6. Mix together breadcrumbs, suet, parsley, and season. Sprinkle over the top.
7. Cook in centre of oven for 1½ hours.

PORK CHOPS PAPRIKA
Serves 4

4 pork chops
1½oz (37gm) cornflour, seasoned
with salt and pepper
2 tablespoons corn oil
1 onion, chopped
1 garlic clove
4oz (100gm) button mushrooms
¾ pint (375ml) beef stock
1 level tablespoon paprika
pepper
1 carton soured cream

1. Coat the chops in cornflour.
Reserve remaining cornflour.
2. Heat oil and fry the chops on
both sides until tender.
3. Remove to a serving dish and
keep warm.
4. Add onion, garlic, mushrooms,
stock, paprika pepper and
remaining cornflour to the pan.
Bring to the boil, stirring.
5. Boil for 3 minutes, stirring all
the time.
6. Remove from the heat and stir
in the soured cream.
7. Pour the sauce around the
chops and serve.

PORK CHOPS WITH ALMONDS
Serves 4

1oz (25gm) soft brown sugar
1 tablespoon French mustard
4 sparerib pork chops
salt and pepper
1oz (25gm) almonds, blanched
and shredded

1. Mix sugar and mustard
together in a paste. Spread over
the chops and season well.
2. Grill on both sides until golden
and tender.
3. Sprinkle with almonds and
grill a little longer until almonds
are lightly browned.

PORK AND PRUNES IN A POT
Serves 4

4oz (100gm) prunes
piece of lemon rind
1lb (½ kilo) lean pork
1½oz (37gm) flour, seasoned
with salt and pepper
1oz (25gm) dripping
½ pint (250ml) stock
1lb (½ kilo) potatoes

1. Preheat oven to moderate, 350
deg F or gas 4 (180 deg C).
2. Put the prunes in a pan with
lemon rind and cover with water.
Cook slowly until tender.
3. Strain, reserving juice, and
discard the stones.
4. Trim the pork and cut into
bite-sized pieces.
5. Roll in seasoned flour.
6. Heat the dripping and fry the
pork until golden.
7. Drain meat well and layer in
the casserole with the prunes.
8. Stir remaining flour from
coating the pork into the dripping
left in the pan.
9. Stir in ½ pint (250ml) prune
juice and mix well.
10. Pour over the pork and
prunes. Add stock.
11. Peel and slice the potatoes,
place over the top of casserole.
12. Cover and cook for 1½ hours
in centre of oven.

SAVOURY FRIED PORK
Serves 4

1lb (½ kilo) shoulder or leg of
pork cut into thin slices
salt and pepper
1 egg, beaten
1 packet sage and onion
stuffing
1oz (25gm) lard

1. Flatten the slices of pork with
a rolling pin and cut into portions.
2. Coat each slice with seasoned,
beaten egg and dry stuffing.
3. Fry in hot lard on both sides
until brown and tender.

COUNTRY PORK CUBES
Serves 4

1½lb (¾ kilo) lean pork
¾ pint (375ml) chicken stock
1 level teaspoon salt
1 small onion, chopped
½oz (12gm) sugar
1oz (25gm) cornflour
3 tablespoons vinegar
3 tablespoons apple juice
1 large cooking apple, cooked
and sliced

1. Cut the pork into 1-inch cubes.
2. Turn into a pan with the stock,
salt and onion.
3. Bring slowly to the boil then
allow to simmer very gently until
pork is tender.
4. In another pan blend the sugar,
cornflour, vinegar and apple juice
to a smooth paste.
5. Strain in the liquid drained
from the meat and stir over a
medium heat until sauce thickens.
6. Add the cubes of pork and the
apple slices.
7. Reheat gently and serve.

RICE WITH SHISH KEBAB
Serves 6

6 tablespoons vegetable oil
8oz (200gm) long-grain rice
1 pint (approximately ½ litre)
stock
12oz (300gm) fillet of pork, cut
into 1-inch cubes
12oz (300gm) gammon, cut into
1-inch cubes
4 onions, cut in eighths
4 green peppers, cut in small
pieces
8 tomatoes, cut in half
salt and pepper

1. Heat 2 tablespoons of oil in a
saucepan.
2. Add rice and fry for a few
minutes, then add stock.
3. Bring to the boil and stir once.
4. Lower heat to simmer. Cover
and cook for 15 minutes.
5. Meanwhile, divide the meats,
onions, green pepper and
tomatoes into six portions.
6. Place alternate pieces on six
skewers.
7. Mix rest of oil and seasoning
together and brush over the
kebabs.
8. Cook under a preheated grill
for 8–10 minutes on each side.
9. Serve on the rice.

PORK FRITTERS
Serves 4

1 large can chopped pork
6oz (150gm) plain flour
pinch of salt
1 egg
just over ¼ pint (125ml) milk
and water
dripping

1. Slice the pork into 12 slices.
2. Sift flour into a bowl with the
salt. Add egg, milk and water.
3. Stir the flour into the egg and
then whisk until free of all lumps.
4. Meanwhile, melt the dripping
into a pan.
5. Dip the slices of meat in the
batter, then put them into the hot
fat.
6. Fry until brown on one side
then fry the other side.
7. Drain well and serve with
tomato sauce.

VEAL CASSEROLE
Serves 4

8oz (200gm) veal escalope,
sliced into thin strips
2oz (50gm) butter
1 small head celery, finely
chopped
1 large onion, sliced
12oz (300gm) new potatoes,
peeled and sliced
¾ pint (375ml) beef stock
¾oz (18gm) flour
salt and pepper

1. Preheat oven to moderate, 350
deg F or gas 4 (180 deg C).
2. Fry the veal strips quickly in
the butter, on all sides. Remove to
an ovenware casserole.
3. Fry the celery and onions
gently in the butter until tender
but not brown.
4. Add to veal and mix in the
potatoes.
5. Add stock to frying pan and
thicken with flour. Season to
taste.
6. Pour into a casserole, cover
and place in centre of oven for 1
hour.

VEAL AND APPLE CASSEROLE
Serves 4

1lb (½ kilo) lean stewing veal,
cut into cubes
1oz (25gm) flour, seasoned with
salt and pepper
1oz (25gm) butter
1 tablespoon oil
1 medium onion, sliced
8oz (200gm) cooking apples
½ pint (250ml) chicken stock
1 teaspoon sugar
1 carton (5oz or 125gm) soured
cream
1 teaspoon chopped parsley

1. Preheat oven to very moderate,
325 deg F or gas 3 (170 deg C).
2. Toss the veal in seasoned flour.
3. Heat butter and oil in a pan,
then fry meat until brown.
4. Add onion and cook for further
2 minutes.
5. Stir in any remaining flour.
Cook for 2 minutes, then spoon
into a 2-pint (1 litre) casserole.
6. Peel apples, remove and discard
core and slice into rings.
7. Lay apple rings on top of meat
and pour stock over. Sprinkle
with sugar.
8. Cover and cook in centre of
oven for 1½ hours until tender.
9. Just before serving, spoon on
soured cream and garnish with
parsley.

FRICASSEE OF VEAL
Serves 4

1½lb (¾ kilo) stewing veal
1 onion
piece of turnip
2 carrots
2 sticks celery
salt and pepper
pinch of mixed dried herbs
1 clove
4 peppercorns
piece of lemon rind
1½ pints (approximately ¾ litre)
stock or water
2oz (50gm) butter
2oz (50gm) flour
juice of ½ a lemon
1 egg yolk
2–3 tablespoons cream
bacon rolls and chopped
parsley to garnish

1. Cut the meat into cubes,
removing any skin and gristle.
2. Dice the prepared onion,
turnip, carrots and celery.
3. Put the meat and vegetables
into a stewpan with the seasoning,
and herbs, spices and lemon rind
tied in a muslin bag.
4. Add stock or water to cover
and simmer in a covered pan for
about 1½ hours.
5. Remove the muslin bag of
spices.
6. Melt the butter in a large
saucepan over a low heat, add the
flour and cook gently for a few
minutes, without browning.
7. Add 1 pint (approximately ½
litre) stock from the veal, bring to
the boil, stirring, and simmer
until the sauce thickens.
8. Season and add the lemon
juice, egg yolk and cream.
9. Put in the strained meat and
vegetables and heat through
without boiling.
10. Serve garnished with bacon
rolls and parsley.

FESTIVE VEAL CASSEROLE
Serves 4

2lb (1 kilo) pie veal
2oz (50gm) butter
4oz (100gm) gammon, diced
1lb (½ kilo) small, pickling
onions
3 tablespoons brandy
2oz (50gm) flour
salt and pepper
1 pint (approximately ½ litre)
stock
1 sprig of parsley and thyme
2 tomatoes, skinned

1. Preheat oven to moderate, 350
deg F or gas 4 (180 deg C).
2. Cut up veal and brown in
butter with gammon.
3. Skin onions and add to meat.
Fry until brown.
4. Warm the brandy, pour into
pan and set alight.
5. Turn all the ingredients into a
casserole. Stir flour into butter
remaining in the pan.
6. Season and add stock, parsley
and thyme.
7. Pour over the meat, add
tomatoes and cook in centre of
oven for 2 hours.

VEAL IN A DISH
Serves 4

12oz (300gm) pie veal
4oz (100gm) suet
3oz (75gm) breadcrumbs
1 teaspoon grated lemon rind
salt and pepper
2 eggs
2 tablespoons gravy
¼ pint (125ml) stock

1. Preheat oven to moderate to
moderately hot, 375 deg F or gas 5
(190 deg C).
2. Mince the veal and add to the
suet.
3. Mix with breadcrumbs, lemon
rind and seasoning.
4. Stir in 1 egg and add the gravy.
5. Blend the other egg with the
stock and set on one side.
6. Put the veal mixture into a
greased pie dish.
7. Bake in centre of oven for 45
minutes.
8. Remove from the oven, pour
egg and stock mixture over and
return to the oven until set.
9. Serve hot.

VEAL ROLLS
Serves 4

2oz (50gm) streaky bacon
4 tablespoons cottage cheese
¼ teaspoon sage
salt and pepper
1 egg
4 slices veal
1 bunch of watercress, finely
chopped
1 teaspoon lemon juice
½ pint (250ml) white sauce (see
Basic recipes, page 100)

1. Preheat oven to moderately
hot, 400 deg F or gas 6 (200 deg C).
2. Chop bacon finely and mix
with the cheese.
3. Season with sage, salt and
pepper.
4. Add beaten egg and stir
thoroughly.
5. Heat gently until mixture
begins to thicken.
6. Spread some mixture on each
piece of veal.
7. Roll each piece carefully and
wrap in foil.
8. Bake in centre of oven for
about 30 minutes.
9. Add watercress and lemon
juice to white sauce. Heat and
check seasoning.
10. Serve rolls and sauce
separately.

CREAMY CURRY
Serves 4

1 large onion, peeled and sliced
1oz (25gm) butter
1½lb (¾ kilo) pie veal, diced
2 large carrots, peeled and diced
2 level teaspoons curry powder
½ pint (250ml) milk
salt and pepper
1 dessert apple, cored and chopped

1. Preheat oven to moderate to moderately hot, 375 deg F or gas 5 (190 deg C).
2. Fry onion in butter until soft. Add veal and continue cooking for a few minutes.
3. Add carrots, curry powder, milk and salt and pepper to taste.
4. Bring to the boil and simmer for 3 minutes.
5. Pour into an ovenware casserole. Lay apple on top, cover and cook in centre of oven for 1 hour, or until tender.
6. Thicken with a little cornflour if liked and serve with boiled rice.

STUFFED BREAST OF VEAL
Serves 4

1½lb (¾ kilo) breast of veal, boned
1 small onion, chopped
2oz (50gm) mushrooms, chopped
1½oz (37gm) butter
3 slices bread
2 tablespoons milk
1 egg
salt and pepper
1 teaspoon chopped parsley

1. Preheat oven to cool, 300 deg F or gas 2 (150 deg C).
2. Lay veal skin side down on a board.
3. Fry the onion and mushrooms gently in the butter.
4. Crumble the bread and soak in the milk.
5. Stir in the onions, mushrooms, butter, egg and salt and pepper.
6. Add the parsley and stuff into the joint.
7. Roll up meat, tie with string and roast in centre of oven, allowing 25 minutes per pound (½ kilo) and 25 minutes over.
8. Baste well during cooking.

BAKED BEAN MINCE
Serves 4

2 tablespoons olive oil
1 large onion, finely chopped
1lb (½ kilo) minced meat
salt and pepper
1 medium can baked beans
parsley
triangles of toast to garnish

1. Heat oil in a frying pan, add onion and cook over a low heat until tender.
2. Add minced meat, season to taste and cook for approximately 15 minutes, stirring occasionally, until the meat is cooked.
3. Add baked beans and thoroughly heat through.
4. Serve immediately, garnished with parsley and triangles of toast.

SHEPHERD'S PIE
Serves 4

1lb (½ kilo) potatoes
2 tablespoons milk
½oz (12gm) butter or margarine
salt and pepper
1 onion
½oz (12gm) dripping
8oz (200gm) cooked meat, minced
little stock
1 teaspoon chopped parsley
¼ teaspoon mixed herbs

1. Preheat oven to moderate to moderately hot, 375 deg F or gas 5 (190 deg C).
2. Boil potatoes and when cooked strain off the water and mash them, stirring in milk, butter or margarine, salt and pepper.
3. Chop or slice onion and fry in dripping.
4. Mix together minced meat, stock, seasoning, parsley and herbs, and add fried onion.
5. Line a pie dish with mashed potato and fill the middle of the dish with meat mixture.
6. Cover the top with remaining mashed potato and mark with a fork.
7. Place in centre of oven for about 15 minutes till well heated through, then brown top under a hot grill.

SAVOURY PIE
Serves 4

1lb (½ kilo) potatoes, cooked
1oz (25gm) butter
1 egg
a little milk
2 large tomatoes
1 large onion
2oz (50gm) mushrooms
1oz (25gm) lard
8oz (200gm) cooked meat, minced

1. Preheat oven to moderately hot, 400 deg F or gas 6 (200 deg C).
2. Cream the potatoes with butter, egg and milk.
3. Skin and slice tomatoes and onion.
4. Slice the mushrooms.
5. Fry the tomatoes, onion and mushrooms together in lard until tender.
6. Layer the potatoes, meat and vegetables in a greased pie dish finishing with a top layer of potatoes.
7. Mark the top with a fork.
8. Bake in centre of oven for 15–20 minutes until golden brown and heated through.

RISOTTO
Serves 4

3oz (75gm) butter or margarine
1 large onion, chopped
4oz (100gm) cooked meat, chopped
8oz (200gm) long-grain rice
1 wineglass white wine
1oz (25gm) mushrooms, chopped
salt and pepper
pinch of nutmeg
pinch of saffron
1 pint (approximately ½ litre) chicken stock
2oz (50gm) cheese, grated

1. Melt butter or margarine in a heavy pan and add onion and meat. Fry gently for 10 minutes.
2. Add rice and cook for about 5 minutes until it begins to brown, stirring all the time.
3. Add wine and stir till it is absorbed by the rice.
4. Stir in mushrooms and season with salt, pepper, nutmeg and saffron.
5. Remove pan from heat and pour in stock, stirring well.
6. Cover the pan and simmer gently till rice is cooked.
7. Stir in the cheese 5 minutes before serving.

Sausages and offal

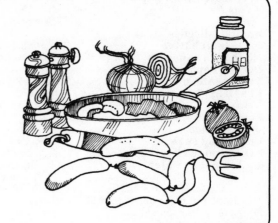

From the following recipes you will be able to produce rich, but not extravagant dishes that will satisfy every member of the family.

SAUSAGE POTATO PIE
Serves 4

1lb (½ kilo) sausages
1 onion, sliced
12oz (300gm) tomatoes
1lb (½ kilo) potatoes, boiled
a little milk
1oz (25gm) butter
salt and pepper
1 teaspoon chopped parsley

1. Preheat oven to hot, 425 deg F or gas 7 (220 deg C).
2. Fry the sausages and then let them cool slightly.
3. Skin most of the sausages (reserve two for garnishing), cut them in half lengthways and put into a pie dish.
4. Fry the onion in the same pan and add the skinned, quartered tomatoes.
5. Meanwhile, mash the potatoes with milk and most of the butter and season well.
6. Pour the onions and tomatoes over the sausages, cover with the potatoes and fork the top to make a pattern.
7. Slice the remaining sausages and place on top. Dot with the rest of the butter.
8. Bake for 15 minutes until the potatoes are brown. Sprinkle with parsley.

SAUSAGE, APPLE AND ONION CASSEROLE
Serves 4

1lb (½ kilo) pork sausages
2oz (50gm) cooking fat
8oz (200gm) onions, chopped
¼ pint (125ml) stock
½ level teaspoon salt
shake of pepper
2 medium cooking apples

1. Preheat oven to moderate, 350 deg F or gas 4 (180 deg C).
2. Brown the sausages in the hot fat then transfer them to a casserole.
3. Fry the onions in the remaining fat in the frying pan until tender but not brown.
4. Sprinkle the onions over the sausages. Add the stock and seasoning.
5. Peel and core the apples. Cut them into rings and place on top of the sausages.
6. Cover and bake in centre of oven for 45 minutes. Serve very hot.

FRENCH POTATOES
Serves 4

2 heaped tablespoons quick-dried onions
½ pint (250ml) stock
1lb (½ kilo) potatoes
1lb (½ kilo) pork sausages, cooked and sliced
salt and pepper
1oz (25gm) butter

1. Preheat oven to moderate to moderately hot, 375 deg F or gas 5 (190 deg C).
2. Place the onions and stock in a saucepan and bring slowly to the boil.
3. Arrange a layer of thinly sliced potato and sausage in a shallow ovenware dish.
4. Season and spoon over some of the stock and onions.
5. Continue filling the dish with these layers, topping with a layer of potato.
6. Dot with the butter and bake in centre of oven for 1 hour.
7. Serve hot.

SPANISH SAUSAGES
Serves 4

1 onion, sliced
2oz (50gm) butter
1lb (½ kilo) sausages
1 green pepper, diced
2 teaspoons salt
1 bayleaf
2 cloves
1 can tomatoes or
tomato juice
1 teaspoon sugar
3 tablespoons flour
6 tablespoons water

1. Fry the onion in hot butter.
2. Add rest of ingredients, except
flour and water. Cover and
simmer for 30 minutes.
3. Mix the flour and water to a
smooth paste.
4. Stir into the mixture and cook,
stirring, until it thickens.
5. Remove the bayleaf and cloves
before serving.

FRANKFURTERS AND SWEETCORN
Serves 4

1 can sweetcorn
1 green pepper
1 large can tomatoes
salt and pepper
12 Frankfurters
butter

1. Preheat oven to moderate, 350
deg F or gas 4 (180 deg C).
2. Put the corn, sliced pepper and
tomatoes in layers in a casserole
dish, finishing with a layer of
corn.
3. Season well, then arrange
the sausages on top.
4. Put some knobs of butter on
top.
5. Bake in centre of oven for 20
minutes.

SAUSAGE AND CHEESE BAKE
Serves 4

8 pork sausages
2 tablespoons prepared
mustard
4oz (100gm) Cheddar cheese
8 bacon rashers
salt and pepper

1. Preheat oven to moderate to
moderately hot, 375 deg F or gas 5
(190 deg C).
2. Slit the sausages lengthways,
but do not cut through. Spread
each slit with mustard.
3. Cut cheese in wedges. Stuff a
piece into each sausage.
4. Wrap each sausage in a bacon
rasher. Fasten bacon in place
with a cocktail stick.
5. Put in a roasting tin, season
and cover. Bake in centre of oven
for 25 minutes.

SAUSAGE SURPRISE
Serves 4

½oz (12gm) cooking fat or
dripping
1lb (½ kilo) pork sausages
4 medium leeks, sliced
1 large can tomatoes
salt and pepper
a few drops Worcestershire
sauce
1 packet quick-dried peas,
cooked as directed

1. Melt the fat in a large pan and
fry the sausages for 20 minutes
until brown.
2. Remove from the pan and keep
warm. Drain away the excess fat
leaving a dessertspoonful in the
pan.
3. Add leeks to the pan and cook
slowly for 10 minutes.
4. Add the canned tomatoes,
seasoning and Worcestershire
sauce, then bring slowly to the
boil.
5. Simmer for a further 5 minutes
then add the drained peas and
reheat.
6. Turn into a hot serving dish
and lay the sausages on top.

SAUSAGEMEAT BALLS WITH SPANISH RICE
(Illustrated on page 35)
Serves 4

1lb (½ kilo) sausagemeat
2oz (50gm) flour, seasoned with
salt and pepper
fat for frying
6oz (150gm) long-grain rice
2oz (50gm) lard
1 onion, chopped
1 small green pepper, chopped
2 sticks celery, chopped
1 small can tomatoes

1. Roll the sausagemeat into
seven or eight balls and then roll
in a little seasoned flour. Fry on
all sides.
2. Boil the rice in plenty of salted
water for about 10–15 minutes,
until tender, then drain it.
3. Melt the lard in a pan, stir in
the onion, pepper and celery and
cook gently for about 15 minutes.
4. Add tomatoes, season well and,
when hot, stir in the rice.
5. Heat through and serve on a
hot dish.
6. Arrange the sausagemeat balls
on the top.

SAUSAGEMEAT PUDDING
Serves 4

1 onion
1 apple
1 tomato
3oz (75gm) breadcrumbs
1lb (½ kilo) sausagemeat
2–3 tablespoons stock
salt and pepper

1. Skin the onion and apple and mince or chop very finely.
2. Skin and chop up the tomato roughly.
3. Turn into a basin with the onion and the apple.
4. Add the breadcrumbs, sausagemeat and just sufficient stock to bind.
5. Season and turn into a greased basin, cover and steam for 1½ hours.

SAVOURY PINWHEELS
Makes 8–10

8oz (200gm) self-raising flour
3oz (75gm) margarine
milk to mix
8oz (200gm) sausagemeat
2 tablespoons sage and onion stuffing

1. Preheat oven to hot, 425 deg F or gas 7 (220 deg C).
2. Sieve the flour and rub in the margarine.
3. Make the mixture to a soft dough by adding milk.
4. Roll out on a floured board to an oblong shape approximately ¼ inch thick.
5. Mix sausagemeat and stuffing and spread over the pastry.
6. Roll up from the long edge like a Swiss roll, then divide into 8 or 10 portions.
7. Place on a greased baking sheet, cut side upwards.
8. Bake in centre of oven for 15 minutes, until browned.

SAUSAGE PANCAKES
Serves 4

1 teaspoon onion, grated
½ pint (250ml) pancake batter (see Basic recipes, page 100)
1 oz (25gm) butter
1oz (25gm) flour
½ pint (250ml) milk
2oz (50gm) cheese, grated
1lb (½ kilo) hot, cooked sausages

1. Add onion to pancake batter and leave to stand for 1 hour.
2. Melt butter in a pan and add flour. Cook for 2 minutes then gradually add milk, stirring constantly. Bring to the boil and stir in cheese.
3. Make pancakes in usual way, spread with cheese sauce and roll up pancakes round the sausages.

LIVER AND BACON PIE
Serves 4

8oz (200gm) fat bacon
8oz (200gm) calf's or pig's liver
8oz (200gm) onions
1½lb (¾ kilo) potatoes
1 teaspoon dried sage
salt and pepper
½ pint (250ml) stock
1oz (25gm) butter

1. Preheat oven to moderately hot, 400 deg F or gas 6 (200 deg C).
2. Cut bacon and liver into small pieces.
3. Slice the onions and peeled potatoes.
4. Grease a pie dish and put a layer of potatoes at the bottom, then a layer of onion and a layer of bacon and liver, sprinkling with the herbs and seasoning. Finish with a layer of potatoes.
5. Pour stock over and dot with butter.
6. Cover and cook in the oven for 1 hour.
7. Remove cover and bake for a further 20–30 minutes until the potatoes are browned.

BACON, LIVER AND MUSHROOM PUDDINGS
Serves 4

2 lean bacon rashers, finely chopped
6oz (150gm) liver, finely chopped
3oz (75gm) mushrooms, chopped
8oz (200gm) self-raising flour
pinch of salt
4oz (100gm) shredded suet
milk to mix

1. Grease four individual basins or moulds.
2. Fry the bacon to extract the fat.
3. Add the liver and mushrooms and cook for 5 minutes.
4. Sift the flour and salt in a bowl.
5. Add the suet and mix well.
6. Stir the liver, bacon and mushroom mixture into the dry ingredients.
7. Add enough milk to give a dropping consistency.
8. Spoon into the basins or moulds.
9. Cover with foil, stand them in a pan of boiling water and steam for 2 hours.
10. Turn out and serve at once with thick brown gravy.

BRAISED LIVER CASSEROLE
(Illustrated on page 35)
Serves 4

1lb (½ kilo) liver
1½oz (37gm) flour
2oz (50gm) dripping
3 onions, chopped
4 bacon rashers, chopped
2 carrots, sliced
1 stick celery, chopped
1 pint (approximately ½ litre) stock

1. Preheat oven to moderate, 350 deg F or gas 4 (180 deg C).
2. Slice and flour the liver and fry it in dripping with the onions and bacon.
3. Remove from the pan and keep hot. Fry carrots and celery.
4. Turn all ingredients into a casserole.
5. Season and add stock.
6. Cook in centre of oven for 45 minutes.
7. Serve with creamed potato.

LIVER WITH ORANGE SLICES
Serves 4

1lb (½ kilo) calf's or lamb's liver
1oz (25gm) flour, seasoned with salt and pepper
1½oz (37gm) butter
1½ teaspoons olive oil
1 onion, finely chopped
2 garlic cloves, very finely chopped
⅛ pint (63ml) stock
2 tablespoons wine
¼ teaspoon Tabasco
1 large orange, peeled and sliced
1oz (25gm) brown sugar
1 tablespoon chopped parsley

1. Trim the liver and cut it into four slices. Dip it in well-seasoned flour.
2. Melt half the butter with 1 teaspoon oil, and fry the liver in it on both sides.
3. Remove it to a hot serving dish and keep it warm.
4. Add the rest of the butter to the frying pan and cook the onion and garlic until soft.
5. Add the stock and the wine. Simmer until it has reduced a little and add Tabasco. Season, if necessary, then pour over the liver.
6. Brush the orange slices with the remaining oil, sprinkle with brown sugar and quickly heat through under the grill.
7. Serve with the liver, sprinkled with parsley.

LIVER MANRAY
Serves 4

1 medium onion
3 tablespoons corn oil
1lb (½ kilo) lamb's liver
1 tablespoon cornflour, seasoned with salt and pepper
½ pint (250ml) beef stock
1 carton soured cream
1 tablespoon white wine vinegar
2 tablespoons capers

1. Peel the onion and slice thinly.
2. Heat the corn oil in a large frying pan and fry the onion until a pale golden brown.
3. Slice the liver and coat in seasoned cornflour.
4. Move the onion to a hot plate and fry the liver for 2 minutes, then remove from pan and keep hot.
5. Add stock to the pan gradually, stirring all the time. Bring to the boil and allow to simmer for 15 minutes.
6. Remove from the heat and stir in the soured cream, wine vinegar and capers.
7. Adjust the seasoning, if necessary. Heat through gently but do not allow to boil.
8. Serve at once, with the onions and liver.

LIVER WITH CREAM SAUCE
Serves 4

1½lb (¾ kilo) calf's liver
2oz (50gm) flour, seasoned with salt and 1 teaspoon paprika pepper
2oz (50gm) butter
1 small onion, finely chopped
1 carton soured cream

1. Wash and dry the liver and cut into slices. Toss in seasoned flour.
2. Heat butter and fry liver until golden. Keep hot.
3. Add onion and cook until tender.
4. Pour off butter and mix in soured cream.
5. Arrange liver on a dish and pour cream sauce over. Serve immediately.

LIVER RAGOUT
Serves 4

1lb (½ kilo) calf's liver
4 tablespoons flour, seasoned with salt and pepper
4 bacon rashers
1oz (25gm) butter
¾ pint (375ml) stock
4oz (100gm) rice
1oz (25gm) sultanas
1 apple
1 teaspoon tomato purée

1. Cut the liver into small pieces and dip in seasoned flour.
2. Dice the bacon.
3. Fry both in the butter until brown.
4. Add stock to pan and bring to the boil, stirring well.
5. Add the rice, sultanas, finely diced or grated apple and tomato purée.
6. Simmer for 20 minutes until the rice is cooked.

GALA SPEARS
Serves 4

4 sheep's kidneys
4 bacon rashers
4 small tomatoes
4 small mushrooms
2oz (50gm) butter, melted
1 tablespoon chopped parsley
1lb (½ kilo) creamed potato

1. Skin, core and halve the kidneys.
2. Remove rinds from bacon and curl each rasher into a roll.
3. Thread on four skewers with tomatoes and mushrooms.
4. Brush with melted butter and grill on all sides.
5. Sprinkle with parsley and serve on a mound of creamed potato or rice.

KIDNEY CASEROLE
Serves 4

6 sheep's kidneys
1½oz (37gm) butter
4oz (100gm) chipolata sausages
10 button onions, blanched
4oz (100gm) mushrooms,
quartered
salt and pepper
1 level dessertspoon flour
¼ pint (125ml) sherry
1 teaspoon tomato purée
½ pint (250ml) stock
1 bayleaf
1 teaspoon chopped parsley

1. Preheat oven to moderate, 350 deg F or gas 4 (180 deg C).
2. Skin the kidneys, cut in half and remove the core.
3. Melt butter and brown first the kidneys and then the sausages quickly. Remove from pan.
4. Put the skinned onions in cold water, bring to the boil, then boil for 2 minutes.
5. Drain and add to the fat remaining in the pan with the mushrooms.
6. Season and cook for 5–6 minutes, stirring occasionally. Remove and keep hot.
7. Add the flour and leave to brown a little.
8. Add the sherry, tomato purée and stock. Return to the heat and stir until it boils.
9. Put the sausages, kidneys, onions and mushrooms in a casserole with bayleaf.
10. Add the sherry sauce and adjust seasoning.
11. Cover and cook in centre of oven for 1 hour.
12. Garnish with parsley.

MUSHROOMS AND KIDNEYS IN A DISH
(Illustrated on page 35)
Serves 4

1lb (½ kilo) kidneys
1 teaspoon chopped onion
2oz (50gm) dripping
1 pint (approximately ½ litre) stock
4oz (100gm) mushrooms, sliced
4 bacon rashers
salt and pepper
1 level teaspoon chopped fresh herbs
5oz (125gm) self-raising flour
2oz (50gm) suet

1. Skin and core the kidneys and cut into small dice.
2. Cook the onion in the dripping until it is tender.
3. Remove from the pan and add the kidney. Brown in the fat.
4. Add the stock and the mushrooms, onion and chopped bacon. Mix in the seasoning and the herbs.
5. Simmer for 20 minutes.
6. Mix the flour with the suet in a bowl and season well.
7. Blend with a little cold water to make dumplings. Shape into four dumplings and set on top of the stew.
8. Cover with a lid and simmer for a further 20 minutes.

KIDNEY GRILL
Serves 4

8 lamb's kidneys
1oz (25gm) butter
8 bacon rashers
1lb (½ kilo) carrots
1 tablespoon sugar
watercress to garnish

1. Skin, core and halve the kidneys. Brush with half the butter melted, and grill until tender.
2. Grill the bacon rashers, then keep them hot.
3. Cook the carrots in boiling, salted water. When just tender, drain well and cut into ½-inch dice.
4. Heat remaining butter and the sugar in a pan. Add the carrots and cook over a moderate heat until lightly browned.
5. Arrange the carrots on a hot dish. Put the kidneys and bacon on the top.
6. Garnish with sprigs of watercress.

KIDNEY OMELETTE
Serves 3–4

4 sheep's kidneys
2oz (50gm) butter
½oz (12gm) flour
salt and pepper
1 small onion, minced
scant ¼ pint (125ml) stock
6 eggs
3 tablespoons milk and water mixed

1. Halve, skin and core the kidneys and chop them up.
2. Melt the butter and add the kidneys.
3. Cook until tender, then remove from pan and keep hot.
4. Add flour and cook until browned but not burnt. Season and add onion and stock.
6. Heat through, then mix in the kidneys.
7. Beat the eggs, add milk and water, season and pour into a hot, buttered, large omelette pan.
8. Stir quickly, then leave to set.
9. Spoon filling over.
10. Fold omelette in three and serve at once.

CURRY OF KIDNEYS
Serves 4

6 sheep's kidneys
1oz (25gm) butter
1 onion
1 small apple
2 teaspoons rice flour
1–2 teaspoons curry powder
squeeze of lemon juice
chutney
salt and pepper
½ pint (250ml) stock
1 tablespoon cream (optional)
lemon and gherkin slices to
garnish

1. Split the kidneys and skin
them, removing the white core.
2. Melt the butter in a small
stewpan.
3. Cook the kidneys and sliced
onion and apple for a few minutes.
4. Add the rice flour and curry
powder and cook these.
5. Add the flavourings and stock,
and stew gently for about 40
minutes, stirring occasionally.
6. Add the cream if used.
7. Dish up the curry with boiled
rice and garnish with lemon and
gherkin.

BAKED STUFFED TRIPE
Serves 4

2lb (1 kilo) dressed tripe
sage and onion stuffing
salt and pepper
½ pint (250ml) stock
3 onions, sliced
2oz (50gm) butter
crisp breadcrumbs

1. Preheat oven to moderate, 350
deg F or gas 4 (180 deg C).
2. Simmer the tripe in a pan of
water for about 15 minutes and
skim the surface free of fat.
3. Drain and dry thoroughly with
a cloth; then spread the stuffing
over the tripe. Roll up and tie
securely.
4. Put into an ovenware dish and
sprinkle with salt and pepper.
5. Add stock and onions.
6. Cover and bake in oven for 1¼
hours.
7. Remove the lid. Brush tripe
with a little melted butter.
8. Sprinkle with the crumbs and
put back into the oven.
9. Raise the heat to hot, 425 deg F
or gas 7 (220 deg C) for 15 minutes.
10. Serve with boiled, diced root
vegetables.

STUFFED HEARTS CASSEROLE
Serves 4

4 sheep's hearts
4oz (100gm) breadcrumbs
1oz (25gm) chopped suet
1 tablespoon chopped parsley
salt and pepper
1 egg, beaten
1oz (25gm) dripping
2 onions, diced
2 carrots, diced
1oz (25gm) flour
¾ pint (375ml) stock

1. Preheat oven to very moderate,
325 deg F or gas 3 (170 deg C).
2. Wash the hearts thoroughly
and cut, through the central
cavity, to make room for the
stuffing.
3. Mix together the breadcrumbs,
suet, parsley, salt and pepper and
bind with beaten egg.
4. Stuff the hearts with this, and
stitch or skewer the top to keep it
in place.
5. Melt the dripping, fry the
onions and carrots and put these
in a casserole dish.
6. Fry the hearts, then put them
in the dish on top of the
vegetables.
7. Make a gravy from the
remaining fat with the flour and
stock.
8. Pour it over the hearts and
cook, covered, in the oven for
about 2 hours.

SWEETBREADS WITH CAPER SAUCE
Serves 4

1lb (½ kilo) sweetbreads
a little flour
1 egg, beaten
2oz (50gm) breadcrumbs
deep fat for frying
2oz (50gm) butter
1 tablespoon capers
2 tablespoons vinegar
salt and pepper

1. Soak the sweetbreads in
lukewarm water and remove
excess fat.
2. Put into a pan of boiling,
salted water.
3. Skim the surface and allow to
simmer for about 15 minutes.
4. Drain and dry in a cloth.
5. Dip the sweetbreads in a little
flour, then coat with egg and
breadcrumbs.
6. Heat the fat and fry the
sweetbreads until golden.
7. Drain thoroughly then melt
the butter.
8. Add the capers, vinegar and
seasoning.
9. Serve the sauce hot with the
fried sweetbreads.

SWEETBREADS ON SKEWERS
Serves 6

1lb (½ kilo) sweetbreads
8oz (200gm) mushrooms
6 bacon rashers
salt and pepper
3oz (75gm) butter
soft breadcrumbs

1. Soak sweetbreads for 2–3
hours in lukewarm water and
remove excess fat.
2. Put into a pan of boiling,
salted water, skim the surface
and simmer for 15 minutes.
3. Drain and dry in a cloth.
4. Quarter the mushrooms and
cut sweetbreads and bacon into
squares.
5. Alternate sweetbreads,
mushroom quarters and bacon on
six small skewers. Sprinkle with
salt and pepper.
6. Melt butter and spread out
breadcrumbs on a large plate.
7. Brush each skewer with melted
butter and roll in breadcrumbs.
8. Grill under a low heat for 15
minutes, turning skewers
frequently.
9. Serve on a bed of boiled rice.

Poultry

Once poultry was eaten on high days and holidays only. Now a chicken, a turkey or a pack of poultry joints provide substantial meals any day of the week.

CRISPY CHICKEN JOINTS
(Illustrated on page 54)
Serves 4

4 chicken joints
1 lemon
salt and pepper
2 eggs
1½oz (37gm) cheese, grated
1½oz (37gm) breadcrumbs
fat for deep frying
4oz (100gm) mushrooms
1oz (25gm) butter
2oz (50gm) almonds, toasted
1 lettuce

1. Sprinkle the chicken joints with lemon juice.
2. Season and leave in a cold place for 2 hours.
3. Dip in beaten egg.
4. Mix together cheese and breadcrumbs and coat the chicken firmly with the mixture.
5. Deep fry until golden. Drain.
6. Fry the sliced mushrooms in the butter and scatter them over the chicken with the almonds.
7. Garnish with lettuce leaves and serve with new potatoes sprinkled with parsley, and peas.

CHEESED CHICKEN
Serves 4

4 chicken joints
1oz (25gm) flour, seasoned with salt and pepper
2½oz (62gm) butter
½oz (12gm) flour
½ pint (250ml) milk
4oz (100gm) Lancashire cheese, crumbled
½ teaspoon prepared mustard
2oz (50gm) fresh, white breadcrumbs

1. Preheat oven to moderately hot, 400 deg F or gas 6 (200 deg C).
2. Toss chicken joints in seasoned flour and place in an ovenware dish.
3. Dot with 2oz (50gm) butter and bake in centre of oven for 20 minutes.
4. Melt rest of butter in a pan. Add flour and cook for 2 minutes. Add milk and stir continuously until sauce thickens.
5. Stir in cheese and season to taste with salt, pepper and mustard. Simmer gently for 2–3 minutes.
6. Drain liquid from cooked chicken into sauce. Stir well, then pour sauce over chicken joints.
7. Sprinkle breadcrumbs over the top and brown under a hot grill.
8. Serve immediately.

OVEN-FRIED CHICKEN
Serves 4

1oz (25gm) flour
1oz (25gm) cheese, grated
1 level teaspoon salt
½ level teaspoon curry powder
4 chicken joints
2oz (50gm) butter

1. Preheat oven to moderately hot, 400 deg F or gas 6 (200 deg C).
2. Mix together flour, cheese, salt and curry powder.
3. Toss the chicken joints in this mixture.
4. Melt the butter in a roasting tin and put the chicken pieces into the tin, skin side down.
5. Bake for 20 minutes on centre shelf.
6. Turn the chicken over and cook for a further 10 minutes until golden and tender.
7. Serve with a green salad and fried potatoes.

CHICKEN WITH LEMON AND ALMONDS
Serves 4

1 lemon
4 chicken joints
3oz (75gm) butter
4oz (100gm) mushrooms
¼ pint (125ml) double cream
2oz (50gm) almonds, blanched and split
salt and pepper
tomatoes and watercress to garnish

1. Cut the lemon in half and squeeze one half over the chicken joints.
2. Melt the butter and slowly fry the chicken on both sides until tender and cooked.
3. Remove from the pan. Arrange on a heatproof dish and keep hot.
4. Slice the mushrooms and lightly fry until tender. Add rest of lemon juice.
5. Pour the cream over the mushrooms and slowly bring just to the boil.
6. Add the almonds, reserving a few for garnish.
7. Season to taste. Pour sauce over the chicken joints.
8. Scatter remaining almonds over the sauce.
9. Cut the tomatoes into waterlilies and grill lightly.
10. Garnish with the tomato waterlilies and watercress.

GRILLED CHICKEN PAPRIKA
Serves 4

1 lemon
4 chicken joints
salt
2oz (50gm) butter, melted
1 level tablespoon sugar
½ level teaspoon paprika pepper
watercress and potato crisps to garnish

1. Squeeze a lemon over the chicken portions and sprinkle lightly with salt.
2. Brush liberally on both sides with melted butter.
3. Place cut side uppermost in the bottom of the grill pan (grid removed) and cook under a medium to low heat for 8–10 minutes.
4. Turn skin side uppermost and sprinkle evenly with mixed sugar and paprika pepper.
5. Continue grilling for a further 10 minutes, or until cooked, brushing frequently with melted butter. Garnish with watercress and potato crisps.

CHICKEN SAUTE WITH TARRAGON
Serves 4

1½oz (37gm) butter
4 chicken joints
salt and pepper
¼ pint (125ml) chicken stock
3 sprigs of fresh tarragon or a good pinch of dried
3 tablespoons double cream
a little chopped tarragon to garnish

1. Melt the butter and fry the chicken portions, turning frequently, until golden brown.
2. Add the seasoning, stock and tarragon.
3. Cover the pan and simmer very gently for 20–25 minutes.
4. Remove the joints and arrange on a serving dish.
5. Add the cream to the liquid remaining in the pan, bring just to the boil, season to taste and strain over the chicken.
6. Sprinkle the dish with chopped tarragon and serve.

GRILLED CHICKEN WITH ALMONDS
Serves 4

4 chicken joints
salt
2½oz (62gm) butter
2oz (50gm) almonds, blanched and shredded
1 tablespoon lemon juice
watercress to garnish

1. Season the joints with salt.
2. Melt the butter in the grill pan (having first removed the grid) and turn the joints in it to coat evenly with butter.
3. With cut side uppermost, grill steadily under a medium heat for about 8–10 minutes, then turn and continue grilling for another 10–15 minutes, until cooked.
4. Baste with butter from the pan, from time to time.
5. Remove joints to a hot dish and keep hot.
6. Put the almonds into the grill pan and grill, turning frequently, until a delicate golden brown. Add the lemon juice and pour over the chicken. Garnish with watercress.

Jellied lamb slices with a green salad (see page 88)   Salad crunch (see page 84)

Crispy bacon salad with yogurt (see page 87)   Cold chicken salad and cherries (see page 90)

Cauliflower cheese with bacon rolls (see page 95)

French onion soup (see page 97)

Succotash (see page 99)

Rice-stuffed green peppers with tomato sauce (see page 97)

PORTUGUESE CHICKEN
Serves 4

1 onion
4oz (100gm) mushrooms
2oz (50gm) butter
4 chicken joints
3 tablespoons dry white wine
(optional)
¼ pint (125ml) rich, brown stock
1½ tablespoons tomato purée
1 chicken bouillon cube
salt and black pepper
1 garlic clove
8oz (200gm) tomatoes, skinned
and halved

1. Preheat oven to moderate to
moderately hot, 375 deg F or gas 5
(190 deg C).
2. Skin and chop the onions finely.
Slice the mushrooms.
3. Melt the butter in a pan and
fry the chicken joints until they
are golden.
4. Add the onions and cook until
tender but not browned.
5. Stir in the mushrooms, wine if
used, stock, tomato purée and the
chicken bouillon cube.
6. Cover with a lid, season well
and cook for 5 minutes.
7. Turn into a casserole which
has been rubbed with garlic.
8. Cover and cook in centre of
oven for 45 minutes.
9. Add the tomatoes after the
casserole has been cooking for 30
minutes.
10. Serve surrounded with a ring
of rice.

PIQUANT CHICKEN
Serves 4

2 tablespoons oil
1oz (25gm) butter
4 chicken joints
1 large onion, finely chopped
2 level tablespoons flour
salt and pepper
4 tablespoons white wine or
cooking sherry
½ pint (250ml) stock or water
4oz (100gm) mushrooms, sliced
1 medium can baked beans in
tomato sauce

1. Preheat oven to moderate to
moderately hot, 375 deg F or gas 5
(190 deg C).
2. Melt oil and butter in a heavy
casserole. Fry the chicken until
golden brown, then remove.
3. Fry the onion until tender.
Blend in the flour.
4. Add seasoning, wine or sherry
and stock or water. Bring to the
boil and cook for 3 minutes.
5. Return the chicken to the
casserole, and cover.
6. Place in centre of oven for 1
hour, or until chicken is tender.
7. Add mushrooms and baked
beans and cook for a further 20
minutes.

CHICKEN NORMANDY
Serves 6

1 roasting chicken (about 3lb or
1½ kilo), jointed
2oz (50gm) butter
1 medium onion, sliced
3 streaky bacon rashers, cut in
strips
3 sticks celery
2 cooking apples
1oz (25gm) flour
¾ pint (375ml) cider
¼ pint (125ml) cream

1. Brown chicken joints in hot
butter. Remove and keep hot.
2. Cook onion, bacon and chopped
celery until just turning brown.
3. Peel, core and dice the apples.
Add to pan and fry for a further 2–
3 minutes.
4. Remove from heat, add flour
and cider. Bring to the boil,
stirring well.
5. Return chicken joints to the
pan, cover and simmer very gently
for about 45 minutes or until
tender.
6. Stir in cream, bring just to the
boil and serve.

DEVILLED CHICKEN
PUDDING
Serves 4

suet crust pastry made with
8oz (200gm) flour (see Basic
recipes, page 100)
½oz (12gm) dripping
3oz (75gm) streaky bacon
4 small chicken joints
½oz (12gm) plain flour, seasoned
with salt and pepper
1 onion, chopped
2 teaspoons prepared mustard
½ pint (250ml) chicken stock
½ teaspoon Worcestershire
sauce

1. Knead dough lightly, then cut
off one third of the pastry for the
lid.
2. Roll out rest of the pastry and
lift into a greased 2½-pint
(approximately 1¼ litre) pudding
basin. Shape into the basin with
fingers.
3. Melt the dripping in a pan. Cut
bacon into small pieces and add to
pan.
4. Toss the chicken joints in
seasoned flour, then brown them
in the dripping.
5. Add onion to the pan and cook
until golden.
6. Mix the mustard with the stock
and Worcestershire sauce.
7. Turn all the ingredients into
the pudding basin.
8. Roll out the remaining dough
and cover pudding basin.
9. Cover and steam for 2½–3 hours.

DEVONSHIRE CHICKEN
Serves 4

1½oz (37gm) bacon fat or butter
4 chicken joints
2oz (50gm) onion, finely
chopped
1 stick celery, sliced
2 streaky bacon rashers,
chopped
1oz (25gm) flour
¼ level teaspoon pepper
¾ pint (375ml) chicken stock
4 tomatoes, skinned and
quartered
cooked peas or chopped parsley
to garnish

1. Preheat oven to moderate, 350
deg F or gas 4 (180 deg C).
2. Melt the fat or butter and fry
the chicken joints slowly for
about 10 minutes, or until golden.
Transfer to a casserole dish.
3. Add the onion, celery and
bacon to the frying pan and cook
gently for several minutes.
4. Sprinkle in the flour and
pepper, stir and cook for 1
minute.
5. Add the stock and stir until
boiling.
6. Add the tomatoes, then pour
over the chicken.
7. Cover, and cook in centre of
oven for 40 to 45 minutes.
8. Serve in the casserole,
garnished with peas or chopped
parsley.

POULET SAUTE
Serves 4

2 tablespoons cooking oil
3oz (75gm) onion, finely
chopped
2oz (50gm) butter
1 roasting chicken (about 3lb or
1½ kilo), jointed
2 tablespoons brandy
1oz (25gm) flour
½ pint (250ml) single cream
1 tablespoon sherry
2 teaspoons lemon juice
salt and pepper

1. Heat the oil in a deep frying
pan and cook the onion gently for
several minutes.
2. Put half the butter into the pan,
allow to melt and add the chicken
pieces.
3. Cover and cook gently, turning
from time to time for about 10
minutes, until golden and cooked.
4. Arrange chicken on a hot
serving dish and keep warm.
5. Add brandy to the pan and
bubble briskly for a minute.
6. Mix the flour with the cream,
add to the pan and stir in the
remaining butter, the sherry and
lemon juice.
7. Season to taste and pour over
the chicken. Serve hot.

CHICKEN PAN FRY
Serves 4

1 chicken (about 3lb or 1½ kilo)
a little flour
fat for frying
12 small onions
2 sticks celery
2–3 carrots
salt and pepper
½ pint (250ml) tomato pulp or
purée

1. Joint the chicken and dredge
the pieces with flour.
2. Fry in hot fat until well
browned. Pour off the fat.
3. Add the sliced onions, celery
and carrots, salt and pepper and
tomato pulp or purée.
4. Simmer gently for 45 minutes
to 1 hour.
5. When the chicken is tender,
remove, and serve with boiled
rice.

ITALIAN CHICKEN
Serves 4

1 roasting chicken (about 3lb or
1½ kilo)
juice of 2 lemons
2 tablespoons olive oil
1 bayleaf
pinch of thyme
pinch of parsley
1 egg, beaten
breadcrumbs
fat for frying
1 egg yolk
¼ pint (125ml) milk
4oz (100gm) small mushrooms,
cooked
salt and pepper
1 teaspoon chopped parsley

1. Joint the chicken. Leave to
soak for about 2 hours in the
juice of 1 lemon and olive oil,
with the bayleaf, thyme and
parsley.
2. Drain the chicken, dip in
beaten egg, coat with
breadcrumbs and fry in hot fat
until golden brown and tender.
Drain.
3. Mix the egg yolk with the milk,
mushrooms, salt and pepper; heat
gently until thickened.
4. Add the remaining lemon juice
and pour the sauce around the
fried chicken.
5. Sprinkle with parsley.

BARCELONAN FRIED CHICKEN
Serves 4

1 chicken (about 3lb or 1½ kilo)
¼ pint (125ml) olive oil
salt and pepper
1 red pepper
1 green pepper
1 large onion
4 bacon rashers
12oz (300gm) long-grain rice
2½ pints (approximately 1¼ litres) stock
2 pineapple rings, diced
chopped chives

1. Joint the chicken and soak it in olive oil seasoned with salt and pepper for about 30 minutes.
2. Cut up the peppers, onion and bacon and fry in 2 tablespoons oil.
3. Add the rice and fry until it becomes opaque.
4. Add chicken stock.
5. Season well and simmer gently until all the liquid is absorbed and the rice is tender.
6. Add the pineapple 5 minutes before the rice finishes cooking.
7. Fry the chicken in hot oil until tender and golden brown.
8. Serve it on the rice, sprinkled with chopped chives.

DEVILLED CHICKEN
Serves 4

1 chicken (about 3lb or 1½ kilo)
1½ tablespoons curry powder
4 tablespoons honey
4 tablespoons French mustard

1. Divide the chicken into 4 pieces. Rub all over with curry powder.
2. Mix together the honey, mustard and remaining curry powder.
3. Brush it over the chicken.
4. Grill the chicken pieces for about 15 minutes, turning them every 5 minutes and basting with the sauce.
5. Serve with boiled rice and a green salad.

CHINESE FRIED CHICKEN
Serves 4

1 chicken (3lb or 1½ kilo), jointed
6 tablespoons soy sauce
6 tablespoons sherry
1 teaspoon sugar
2 spring onions
flour
deep fat for frying

1. Soak the chicken pieces in the soy sauce, sherry, sugar and chopped onions for about 1 hour.
2. Drain them and coat each piece in flour.
3. Fry in hot fat until golden. Drain.
4. Serve with boiled rice flavoured with a little soy sauce and sherry.

CHICKEN AND MUSHROOM PIE
Serves 4

1 chicken (about 3lb or 1½ kilo)
2oz (50gm) plain flour
4oz (100gm) mushrooms
2 onions
4oz (100gm) bacon
a little dripping
½ pint (250ml) giblet stock
salt and pepper
8oz (200gm) bought puff pastry (or see Basic recipes, page 100)
1 egg, beaten

1. Preheat oven to hot, 450 deg F or gas 8 (230 deg C).
2. Joint the chicken and flour the pieces.
3. Cut up the mushrooms, onions and bacon.
4. Fry in dripping until just beginning to colour, then remove from the fat.
5. Fry the chicken joints and put them in a pie dish with the other fried ingredients.
6. Add 2 teaspoons flour to the fat, then gradually add the stock and bring to the boil.
7. Season well and pour over the ingredients in the pie dish. Cool.
8. Cover with pastry, brush with egg and cook in centre of oven for 45 minutes. Reduce the temperature to moderate to moderately hot, 375 deg F or gas 5 (190 deg C) after 20 minutes of cooking. Serve hot.

PAELLA
Serves 4

1 oven-ready chicken (about 3lb or 1½ kilo), jointed
3 tablespoons olive oil
1 onion, peeled and chopped
8oz (200gm) long-grain rice
½ level teaspoon saffron
¾ pint (375ml) chicken stock
1 garlic clove, crushed
salt and pepper
2oz (50gm) shrimps
1 packet (4oz or 100gm) frozen peas
1 red pepper, seeded and chopped

1. Cut the flesh off the chicken bones and cut into small pieces, then fry in oil until golden. Remove from pan and keep hot.
2. Fry the onion until tender, add the rice and cook until transparent. Do not brown.
3. Add the saffron, chicken stock, garlic, salt, pepper and bring to the boil.
4. Add the shrimps, peas, chicken and pepper. Cover and simmer for 15–20 minutes.
5. Add a little more stock if necessary and stir occasionally.
6. Check seasoning and serve immediately.

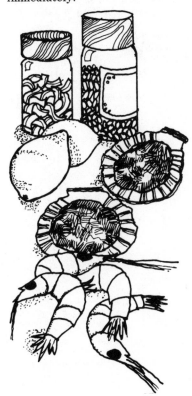

PINEAPPLE CHICKEN GRILL
Serves 4

1 small can pineapple cubes
1 tablespoon lemon juice
1 chicken (about 3lb or 1½ kilo),
split in half
2oz (50gm) butter
salt
finely chopped mint and sprigs
of fresh mint to garnish

1. Drain the syrup from the
pineapple cubes. Add the lemon
juice to it and pour over the
chicken. Leave to soak for 1 hour.
2. Melt the butter in a small pan.
3. Drain and dry the chicken.
Brush liberally with butter on
both sides and sprinkle with salt.
4. Arrange skin-side down in grill
pan (grid removed) and place 5–6
inches below source of heat. Grill
gently for 12–15 minutes.
5. Turn, brush with butter and
continue grilling gently, with
occasional applications of butter,
for a further 12–15 minutes.
6. Meanwhile, add drained and
dried pineapple cubes to the
butter remaining in a small pan
and toss and heat together for
several minutes.
7. Serve chicken halves on a flat
dish, arrange pineapple cubes
between them.
8. Sprinkle with finely chopped
mint and garnish with sprigs of
mint.

APPLE-GLAZED STUFFED CHICKEN
Serves 4

4oz (100gm) fresh breadcrumbs
1 small onion, chopped
1 stick celery, chopped
2 tablespoons chopped parsley
2oz (50gm) blanched almonds
1 teaspoon salt
1 teaspoon mixed herbs
2 tablespoons water
3oz (75gm) butter, melted
1 roasting chicken (about 3lb or
1½ kilo), split in half
1 level tablespoon cornflour
¼ teaspoon ground ginger
½ pint (250ml) sweetened apple
juice (not canned)
watercress to garnish

1. Preheat oven to moderately
hot, 400 deg F or gas 6 (200 deg C).
2. Put breadcrumbs, onion, celery,
parsley and 1oz (25gm) chopped
almonds into a bowl.
3. Add salt, mixed herbs, water
and half the butter and stir well.
4. Wipe chicken thoroughly with
a damp cloth, then stuff insides
with the mixture.
5. Arrange cut side down in a
roasting tin.
6. Cover and roast for 1 hour.
7. Combine the cornflour and
ginger in a saucepan and
gradually add the apple juice.
8. Cook over a moderate heat,
stirring constantly and bring to
the boil.
9. Add rest of almonds, shredded.
Spoon some of this mixture over
the chicken halves to serve.
10. Garnish with watercress.
Serve the remaining glaze
separately.

BARBECUED CHICKEN GRILL
Serves 4

2oz (50gm) butter
1 chicken (about 3lb or 1½ kilo),
split into half
4 tablespoons malt vinegar
1 tablespoon Worcestershire
sauce
1 tablespoon tomato purée
1 level tablespoon brown sugar
1 teaspoon finely grated onion
1 teaspoon paprika pepper
½ teaspoon salt
watercress to garnish

1. Melt butter in a small
saucepan and brush it liberally all
over the chicken.
2. Arrange chicken skin-side
down in the grill pan (grid
removed), place 5–6 inches below
source of heat and grill gently for
12–15 minutes.
3. Meanwhile, add the remaining
ingredients to the butter in the
saucepan and simmer for 2
minutes.
4. Turn the chicken over, brush
with the barbecue sauce and
continue grilling gently, with
frequent applications of sauce,
for a further 12–15 minutes.
5. Pour the remaining sauce over
the chicken and serve garnished
with watercress, accompanied by
crusty rolls and butter.

CHICKEN GOUJON
Serves 4

8oz (200gm) raw chicken meat
1 large egg, beaten
1 packet parsley and thyme
stuffing
oil for frying

1. Cut chicken into thin strips
about 2 inches long.
2. Dip into beaten egg and coat
with dry stuffing mix.
3. Deep fry until crisp and golden.
Drain on absorbent paper.
4. Serve hot with a tomato sauce
or cold with salad.

FRICASSEE OF CHICKEN
Serves 6

1 boiling chicken (about 3lb or 1½ kilo)
2 pints (approximately 1 litre) water
2 carrots
2 onions
1 level teaspoon salt
2–3 strips lemon rind
a few mushroom stalks
sprig of parsley
2oz (25gm) butter
2oz (25gm) flour
½ pint (250ml) milk
salt and pepper

1. Steam the chicken for 1½ hours.
2. Take the chicken flesh off its carcass, remove the skin and cut up chicken into neat pieces.
3. Make stock by boiling all the bones with the water, carrots and onions. Simmer for 1½ hours.
4. Put the chicken meat into a casserole. Add the salt, lemon rind, mushroom stalks, parsley and strained stock.
5. Simmer for 1½ hours until chicken is completely tender.
6. Strain off liquid and keep the chicken hot.
7. Melt the butter in a pan, add the flour and cook for 1 minute. Remove from heat and blend in ½ pint (250ml) stock and the milk.
8. Stir over gentle heat for 2 minutes. Season well.
9. Add chicken and heat carefully until piping hot.
10. Serve on a hot dish with peas and boiled potatoes.

CHICKEN AND RED PEPPERS
Serves 4

1 roasting chicken (3lb or 1½ kilo)
dripping
2 onions
stock or water
piece of orange peel
2 red peppers
1lb (½ kilo) tomatoes
1 garlic clove, crushed
salt and pepper
pinch of herbs
8oz (200gm) long-grain rice

1. Brown the chicken in dripping with the sliced onions.
2. When it is golden brown all over, add enough stock or water to cover.
3. Add orange peel and simmer until tender, about 40 minutes. Strain stock and reserve. Keep chicken hot.
4. Cut up the peppers and tomatoes.
5. Fry in hot fat, season with garlic, salt, pepper and herbs and cook until tender.
6. Cook the rice in the chicken stock, drain, and put on a dish.
7. Carve the chicken, arrange on the rice and cover with the tomatoes and peppers.

SOMERSET CHICKEN CASSEROLE
Serves 4–6

1 chicken (3lb or 1½ kilo)
8oz (200gm) sausagemeat
1 tablespoon flour, seasoned with salt and pepper
1½oz (37gm) dripping or bacon fat
1 small onion, finely chopped
2oz (50gm) mushroom stalks, chopped
¼ pint (125ml) dry cider
small new potatoes and/or button onions or mushrooms to garnish

1. Preheat oven to moderate, 350 deg F or gas 4 (180 deg C).
2. Stuff the neck end of the chicken with sausagemeat and secure the skin flap with a small skewer.
3. Dust the chicken with the seasoned flour.
4. Meanwhile, melt the fat in a flameproof casserole over a gentle heat and fry the onion until soft but not browned.
5. Add the chicken and brown lightly all over.
6. Add the mushroom stalks and cider.
7. Cover tightly and cook in centre of oven for 1 hour.
8. Add the new potatoes and/or onions or mushrooms 20 minutes before the end of cooking time.
9. Replace in the oven and continue cooking. Serve in the casserole.

COUNTRY CHICKEN
Serves 6–8

1 chicken (about 4lb or 2 kilo)
salt and pepper
4oz (100gm) sausagemeat
1 tablespoon fresh
breadcrumbs
1 chicken liver, chopped
1 tablespoon chopped parsley
2½oz (75gm) butter
4oz (100gm) lean bacon, cut
into small pieces
1lb (½ kilo) potatoes, cut into
small cubes
1 teaspoon chopped parsley

1. Preheat oven to moderate, 350
deg F or gas 4 (180 deg C).
2. Remove giblets from body
cavity and season chicken inside
and out with salt and pepper.
3. Mix together sausagemeat,
breadcrumbs, chicken liver and
parsley for the stuffing and insert
into the neck end of the bird,
carefully replacing the flap of skin
under the wings.
4. Melt the butter in a large,
flameproof casserole and lightly
brown the chicken all over.
5. Add the bacon and cover and
cook over a very gentle heat for
15 minutes.
6. Baste the chicken, add the
potatoes, turning them in the fat
and replace the lid.
7. Transfer to centre of oven for
40–50 minutes.
8. Serve in the casserole,
sprinkling the potatoes with
parsley.

MUSHROOM AND CHICKEN PIE
Serves 4

1 boiling chicken, (about 3lb or
1½ kilo) cooked and jointed
1 carrot, shredded
2 large onions, sliced
2oz (50gm) fresh peas
salt and pepper
½oz (12gm) cornflour
¼ pint (125ml) chicken stock
4 streaky bacon rashers,
chopped
4oz (100gm) mushrooms
shortcrust pastry made with
8oz (200gm) flour (see Basic
recipes, page 100)

1. Preheat oven to moderately
hot, 400 deg F or gas 6 (200 deg C).
2. Put the chicken joints into a
pie dish.
3. Add the carrot, onions, peas
and seasoning.
4. Blend the cornflour with the
stock and pour over the chicken.
5. Top with the bacon and sliced
mushrooms.
6. Roll out the pastry and make a
lid to the pie.
7. Bake in centre of oven for 20
minutes, then reduce heat to very
moderate, 325 deg F or gas 3 (170
deg C) for a further 15–20 minutes.

CHICKEN CROQUETTES
Serves 4

1 packet (½ pint or 250ml) bread
sauce mix
¼ pint (125ml) milk
8oz (200gm) cooked chicken,
chopped finely or minced
pinch of nutmeg
1 level tablespoon cornflour
1 egg, beaten
breadcrumbs for coating
oil for frying

1. Make up bread sauce as
directed on the packet but use
only ¼ pint (125ml) milk.
2. Stir in the chicken and nutmeg.
Leave until cold.
3. Divide into four portions and
shape into round, flat cakes.
4. Coat with cornflour, then with
egg and breadcrumbs.
5. Heat the oil in a deep pan. Fry
for 2–3 minutes until golden
brown. Drain on absorbent paper.
6. Serve at once.

CHICKEN RISOTTO
Serves 4

12oz (300gm) leftover chicken
bouquet garni
salt and pepper
2–3 onions
4oz (100gm) mushrooms
1½oz (37gm) dripping
12oz (300gm) long-grain rice
4 bananas
2oz (50gm) butter
grated cheese

1. Cut the chicken into neat
pieces.
2. Boil the bones in water with
the bouquet garni and seasoning
to make 1½ pints (approximately
¾ litre) stock.
3. Cut up the onions and half the
mushrooms.
4. Fry in the dripping, then add
the rice and fry this until opaque.
5. Add the boiling stock and some
salt.
6. Cook gently until the liquid is
absorbed and the rice tender.
7. Do not stir while cooking, but
fork over gently.
8. Lay the chicken on top of the
rice for about 10 minutes, to heat
through.
9. Fry the remaining mushrooms
and the bananas in butter.
10. Put the rice and chicken in a
heatproof dish, sprinkle with
cheese and brown under the grill.
11. Serve garnished with
mushrooms and bananas and
accompanied by a green salad.

SCALLOPED CHICKEN
Serves 4

1½lb (¾ kilo) cooked chicken
8oz (200gm) tomatoes, skinned
and sliced
4oz (100gm) soft breadcrumbs
2 tablespoons chopped parsley
2 level teaspoons salt
4 eggs
1 pint (approximately ½ litre)
chicken stock

1. Preheat oven to moderate, 350
deg F or gas 4 (180 deg C).
2. Chop the chicken into bite-
sized pieces.
3. Arrange layers of chicken,
tomatoes, breadcrumbs and
parsley in a greased baking dish.
4. Mix salt and beaten eggs
together, then add chicken stock.
Pour over the chicken.
5. Stand the dish in a pan of hot
water in centre of oven for 1 hour,
or until set.

CREAMED CHICKEN WITH RICE
Serves 4

1 cold cooked chicken (about
3lb or 1½ kilo)
2oz (50gm) butter
1oz (25gm) flour
1 bouillon cube
½ pint (250ml) chicken stock
grated rind of 1 lemon
1 tablespoon lemon juice
2 tablespoons chopped parsley
6oz (150gm) long-grain rice
2 tablespoons cream

1. Skin chicken, remove flesh
from bones and chop roughly.
2. Melt 1oz (25gm) butter, add
flour and bouillon cube and mix
well.
3. Remove from heat and
gradually add stock. Return pan
to heat, bring to boil and mix in
lemon rind, lemon juice, parsley
and chicken pieces.
4. Cover and leave on a very low
heat.
5. Meanwhile, wash rice and cook
in fast boiling, salted water for
about 10–15 minutes.
6. Drain well and return to the
pan with rest of butter. Shake
over a low heat until the excess
moisture is absorbed.
7. Reheat chicken mixture and
add cream.
8. Pour into a shallow dish and
surround with a border of rice.

CHICKEN PATTIES
Serves 6

8oz (200gm) bought puff pastry
(or see Basic recipes, page 100)
1 egg, beaten
2oz (50gm) mushrooms
a little milk or butter
4oz (100gm) cooked chicken,
chopped
1 teaspoon lemon juice
2 teaspoons chopped parsley
¼ pint (125ml) thick white sauce
(see Basic recipes, page 100)

1. Preheat oven to hot, 450 deg F
or gas 8 (230 deg C).
2. Roll out the pastry ½ inch thick.
Cut out six rounds, marking the
middles with a smaller cutter so
that they can be easily removed
after baking.
3. Brush with egg and bake on
second shelf of oven for 15
minutes.
4. Cut out the tops, scoop the
uncooked part from inside the
patties and put them back in the
oven for a few minutes to dry.
5. Cook the mushrooms in a little
milk or butter.
6. Allow to cool, then chop and
mix with the remaining
ingredients.
7. When pastry cases are cold,
fill them with the chicken
mixture. Put back the lids. Serve
hot or cold.

CHICKEN AND BACON FRIES
Serves 4

1oz (25gm) butter
1oz (25gm) flour
¼ pint (125ml) milk
salt and pepper
6oz (150gm) cooked chicken,
minced
2oz (50gm) bacon, minced
little grated lemon rind
1 egg, beaten
4oz (100gm) fresh breadcrumbs

1. Melt the butter in a pan and
add the flour.
2. Beat in the milk and return to
the heat.
3. Season and cook until
thickened.
4. Add chicken and bacon and
mix in the lemon rind.
5. Spread on a plate and when
cold divide into eight pieces.
6. Coat with egg and breadcrumbs
and deep fry until golden. Drain.
7. Serve piping hot.

CROUSTADES OF CHICKEN
Serves 4

1 stale loaf
1oz (25gm) butter
1oz (25gm) flour
½ pint (250ml) milk
salt and pepper
6oz (150gm) cooked chicken
2oz (50gm) mushrooms, cooked
fat for deep frying

1. Cut the loaf into 3-inch cubes
and scoop out the centre of each.
2. Melt the butter, stir in the
flour and cook for a few minutes.
Beat in the milk and cook,
stirring, until thickened.
3. Season and add the chopped
chicken and mushrooms.
4. Heat the fat until hot, fry the
croustades golden brown, drain
well and fill them with hot
chicken mixture.

CHICKEN PICNIC PATTIES
Serves 4

2 onions
2 bacon rashers
dripping for frying
8oz (200gm) cooked chicken,
minced
2oz (50gm) flour, seasoned with
salt and pepper
⅛ pint (63ml) stock
salt and pepper
shortcrust pastry made with
6oz (150gm) flour (see Basic
recipes, page 100)
1 egg, beaten

1. Preheat oven to hot, 425 deg F
or gas 7 (220 deg C).
2. Slice the onions and cut up the
bacon. Fry both in dripping.
3. Add the chicken, seasoned
flour and stock. Season well.
4. Allow to cook for a few
minutes, then leave to cool.
5. Roll pastry out and line some
patty tins, reserving enough
pastry to cover patties.
6. Fill each one with chicken
mixture.
7. Damp the edges and cover
each with pastry.
8. Brush with egg and bake on
second shelf down of oven for 20–
25 minutes. Serve hot or cold.

CHICKEN FLAN
Serves 6–8

shortcrust pastry made with
6oz (150gm) flour (see Basic
recipes, page 100)
2oz (50gm) butter
1½oz (37gm) flour
1 pint (approximately ½ litre)
milk
salt and pepper
1lb (½ kilo) cooked chicken,
diced
4 tomatoes
2oz (50gm) cheese, grated
parsley to garnish

1. Preheat oven to moderately
hot, 400 deg F or gas 6 (200 deg C).
2. Roll out pastry and line a
10-inch (25cm) flan ring or
sandwich tin.
3. Prick base, line with
greaseproof paper and some
baking beans.
4. Bake on centre shelf of oven
for 15 minutes.
5. Remove beans, flan ring and
paper and continue cooking for a
further 5 minutes.
6. Melt the butter, blend in flour
and cook for 2 minutes.
7. Mix in milk smoothly. Cook for
2–3 minutes over a moderate heat
until sauce thickens. Season to
taste.
8. Fill the flan with the chicken
and pour the sauce over.
9. Slice the tomatoes and arrange
round the edge of flan.
10. Sprinkle with cheese and grill
for 5 minutes until golden.
Garnish with parsley and serve
hot.

CHICKEN TART
Serves 4

shortcrust pastry made with
4oz (100gm) flour (see Basic
recipes, page 100)
1 onion, chopped
2oz (50gm) butter
½ head of celery
1oz (25gm) flour
½ pint (250ml) milk
salt and pepper
4oz (100gm) cooked chicken,
chopped
2oz (50gm) cheese, grated

1. Preheat oven to moderately
hot, 400 deg F or gas 6 (200 deg C).
2. Roll out the pastry and line a
7-inch (18cm) flan case.
3. Prick base and line with
greaseproof paper. Fill with
baking beans.
4. Bake for 10 minutes on the
centre shelf, remove beans and
paper and cook for a further 5
minutes.
5. Cook onion gently in half the
butter.
6. Thinly slice the celery, add to
onion and cook gently.
7. Melt rest of butter, add flour
and blend in the milk. Season and
cook until thick, then pour over
onion and celery.
8. Add chicken and half the
cheese and pour into the pastry
case.
11. Sprinkle with rest of cheese
and brown gently under the grill.
Serve cold.

QUICK CHICKEN CURRY
Serves 4

1oz (25gm) butter
6oz (150gm) mushrooms
salt
1lb (½ kilo) cooked chicken
1 packet curry sauce mix
4oz (100gm) boiled long grain
rice (raw weight)
chutney

1. Heat butter in a pan, add sliced
mushrooms, season with salt and
simmer for 2 minutes.
2. Lightly chop chicken into
½-inch pieces and mix with
mushrooms.
3. Prepare sauce following
instructions on packet, then add
mushroom and chicken mixture.
4. Serve curry with rice,
accompanied by chutney.

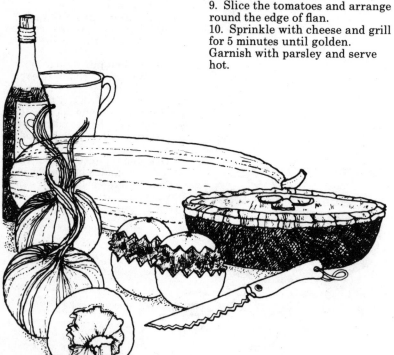

DEEP SOUTH CASSEROLE
Serves 4–6

12oz (300gm) cooked chicken,
thinly sliced
8oz (200gm) frozen mixed
vegetables
½oz (12gm) cornflour
1 packet (1 pint or
approximately ½ litre)
asparagus soup mix
1 pint (approximately ½ litre)
water
1 teaspoon Worcestershire
sauce
2oz (50gm) cheese, grated
2oz (50gm) fresh, white
breadcrumbs
tomato slices and parsley to
garnish

1. Preheat oven to moderate to
moderately hot, 375 deg F or gas 5
(190 deg C).
2. Arrange the chicken and mixed
vegetables in layers in a casserole.
3. Mix together cornflour and
soup mix. Gradually stir in the
water and Worcestershire sauce
and bring to the boil, stirring.
4. Pour over ingredients in
casserole.
5. Mix the cheese and
breadcrumbs together and
sprinkle over the top of the
casserole.
6. Bake on centre shelf of oven
for 25 minutes.
7. Grill for a few minutes to
brown the top.
8. Garnish with tomato and
parsley.

ORANGE-SAUCED DUCK
(Illustrated on page 54)
Serves 4

1 oven-ready duckling
2oz (50gm) flour, seasoned with
salt and pepper
3 tablespoons olive oil
1 garlic clove
¾ pint (375ml) chicken stock
3 oranges, halved
pinch of mixed herbs
1 tablespoon Cognac (optional)
8oz (200gm) cooked long-grain
rice (raw weight)
1 small packet frozen peas
watercress
few lettuce leaves
1 orange, peeled and cut into
segments
10 glacé cherries, halved

1. Preheat oven to very moderate,
325 deg F or gas 3 (170 deg C).
2. Remove giblets, wash body and
dry thoroughly.
3. Joint duckling into 4 portions
and coat in seasoned flour.
4. Fry until browned in hot oil to
which crushed garlic has been
added.
5. Remove joints and drain well
on kitchen paper.
6. Add flour to oil and make roux.
Gradually add stock and cook
over a low heat to make the
sauce.
7. Add the orange juice, scraped
out orange pulp (from the 3
oranges), herbs and season well.
8. Place joints in an ovenware
dish, coat with sauce and bake in
centre of oven for about 1½ hours
or until tender.
9. Remove the duckling portions
from the sauce and add Cognac, if
used.
10. Place the portions on a bed of
cooked rice and peas, spoon a
little sauce over and serve the
remainder of the sauce separately.
11. Garnish with half orange
shells filled with sprigs of
watercress.
12. Accompany with an orange
salad, made with lettuce leaves,
orange segments and glacé
cherries.

DUCKLING WITH FRUIT STUFFING
Serves 4

1 oven-ready duckling
¾ level teaspoon salt
1 eating apple, peeled and
chopped
2 sticks celery, diced
1 medium onion, chopped
2oz (25gm) butter
10 slices currant bread, diced
¼ teaspoon chopped thyme

1. Preheat oven to very moderate,
325 deg F or gas 3 (170 deg C).
2. Clean, wash and drain
duckling. Dry skin gently with
paper towelling.
3. Sprinkle with ½ teaspoon salt.
4. Fry apple, celery and onion in
butter until apple is tender.
5. Add bread and thyme and
remaining salt; mix carefully.
6. Fill duckling loosely with
stuffing mixture.
7. Close neck opening with a
skewer.
8. Cover top of duckling with foil
and tie legs together loosely.
9. Place duckling on rack in
roasting tin.
10. Roast until drumstick meat is
tender, allowing 25–30 minutes
per pound (½ kilo).

PINEAPPLE TURKEY LOAF
Serves 6–8

3 pineapple rings, drained and halved
12oz (300gm) cooked turkey, minced
4oz (100gm) fresh white breadcrumbs
1 small onion, minced or finely grated
3oz (75gm) mushrooms, coarsely chopped
½ level teaspoon celery salt
1 rounded tablespoon chopped parsley
2 large eggs, beaten
¼ pint (125ml) milk
2 teaspoons Worcestershire sauce
salt and pepper
fried almonds and watercress to garnish

1. Preheat oven to moderate, 350 deg F or gas 4 (180 deg C).
2. Arrange pineapple in the bottom of a well greased 2-lb (1 kilo) loaf tin.
3. Combine turkey, breadcrumbs, onion, mushrooms, celery salt and parsley with the eggs and milk, then stir in Worcestershire sauce and seasoning to taste.
4. Turn into the prepared loaf tin, smooth top with a knife and bake in centre of oven for 1 hour, or until firm.
5. Turn out on to a warm dish.
6. Garnish with fried almonds and watercress sprigs and serve with tomato sauce. Alternatively, serve it cold with salad or as a sandwich filling.

TURKEY RISOTTO
Serves 4

2oz (50gm) butter or 2 tablespoons turkey fat
1 large onion, peeled and chopped
1 small garlic clove, peeled and crushed
8oz (200gm) long-grain rice
1 pint (approximately ½ litre) turkey stock or water
4 large tomatoes, skinned and chopped
1 bayleaf
12oz (300gm) cooked turkey, cut into fairly small pieces.
grated Parmesan cheese

1. Melt fat in a pan, add onion and garlic and cook slowly until pale golden.
2. Stir in rice and fry for 5 minutes or until lightly browned.
3. Add stock or water, tomatoes and bayleaf.
4. Cover pan and simmer for 20–25 minutes, by which time the rice grains should be just tender and most of the liquid absorbed.
5. Add turkey, stir well, cover pan and heat through slowly for a further 10–12 minutes.
6. Pile on to a heated plate. Serve with Parmesan cheese.

TURKEY TWISTS
Serves 4

1oz (25gm) butter
1oz (25gm) flour
¼ pint (125ml) stock
salt and pepper
lemon juice
4oz (100gm) cooked turkey, minced
2oz (50gm) ham, minced
1oz (25gm) mushrooms, minced
1 tablespoon top of the milk
1 egg, beaten
fine breadcrumbs
fat for frying

1. Melt the butter, stir in the flour and gradually mix in the stock.
2. Bring to the boil, season and add a few drops of lemon juice.
3. Add the turkey, ham, mushrooms and milk and let the mixture cool.
4. Form into cigar shapes and brush with beaten egg.
5. Coat with breadcrumbs and fry in hot fat until golden brown. Drain.
6. Serve hot with a tomato sauce or cold with salad.

TURKEY FRICASSEE
Serves 4

12oz (300gm) cooked turkey
1oz (25gm) butter
1oz (25gm) flour
½ pint (250ml) stock or milk
salt and pepper
2 egg yolks
parsley, bacon rolls and triangles of fried bread to garnish

1. Cut the turkey into neat pieces.
2. Melt the butter and add the flour. Cook for a minute over a low heat.
3. Gradually add the stock or milk and bring to the boil.
4. Season well and beat in the egg yolks.
5. Add the pieces of turkey and heat slowly until really hot. (Do not boil.)
6. Serve garnished with parsley, bacon rolls and triangles of fried bread.

TURKEY PANCAKES

(Illustrated on page 54)
Serves 4

6oz (150gm) plain flour
pinch of salt
1 pint (approximately ½ litre)
milk
1 egg
½oz (12gm) butter
2 level teaspoons
curry powder
salt and pepper
12oz (300gm) cooked turkey
fat for frying

1. Sieve 4oz (100gm) flour and the
salt into a bowl.
2. Mix with ½ pint (250ml) milk
and egg to form a smooth batter.
Beat well.
3. Melt the butter in a pan, add
the curry powder and rest of
flour. Cook slowly for about 8
minutes.
4. Add rest of milk, cook the
sauce for a few minutes, then
season.
5. Add the turkey, chopped in
small pieces, heat through and
keep hot.
6. Melt the fat in a frying pan and
make the pancakes.
7. Fill with the turkey mixture
and roll up.

HAM AND TURKEY LOAF

Serves 6–8

4oz (100gm) cornflakes,
crushed
8oz (200gm) ham, cooked and
minced
8oz (200gm) cooked turkey or
chicken, minced
1 medium onion, minced
5 level tablespoons tomato
ketchup
4 eggs
1 level teaspoon dry mustard
¼ level teaspoon ground cloves
salt and pepper
1½oz (37gm) soft brown sugar
1 tablespoon water

1. Preheat oven to moderate to
moderately hot, 375 deg F or gas 5
(190 deg C).
2. Put cornflakes, ham, turkey or
chicken and onion into a large
basin.
3. Add tomato ketchup, eggs,
mustard, cloves, salt and pepper
and mix together well.
4. Put into a greased, lined 2-lb
(1 kilo) loaf tin.
5. Mix together brown sugar and
water and spread over the top of
the loaf.
6. Bake in centre of oven for
about 45 minutes.
7. Serve hot with tomato sauce or
cold with salad.

TURKEY IN CIDER JELLY

Serves 4–8

1lb (½ kilo) cooked turkey, cut
into small cubes
½oz (12gm) gelatine
½ pint (250ml) boiling water
¼ pint (125ml) cider

1. Fill 8 individual fancy moulds
or custard cups with turkey.
2. Dissolve gelatine in boiling
water and add cider. Pour into
moulds or cups and leave in a cold
place until firm and set.
3. Turn out of the moulds on to a
bed of lettuce and serve with
tomato salad.

BLANQUETTE OF TURKEY

Serves 4

1½oz (37gm) butter or
margarine
1oz (25gm) flour
¾ pint (375ml) chicken stock
salt and pepper
pinch of mace
1 egg yolk
2 tablespoons cream
12oz (300gm) cooked turkey

1. Melt butter or margarine in a
saucepan and add flour. Cook for
2 minutes.
2. Remove pan from heat and add
stock gradually, beating all the
time.
3. Return to heat and bring to the
boil, stirring well. Season with
salt, pepper and mace.
4. Remove pan from heat and add
egg yolk and cream, mixing them
in quickly.
5. Add turkey cut in small, neat
pieces. Reheat mixture without
allowing it to boil.
6. Serve with bacon rolls, grilled
tomatoes and croûtons of toast.

TURKEY CANAPES

Serves 6

5oz (125gm) butter
1 tablespoon flour
¼ pint (125ml) Madeira
½ pint (250ml) turkey or chicken
stock
salt and pepper
1¼lb (¾ kilo) cooked turkey,
chopped
1oz (25gm) green olives, sliced
juice of half lemon
6 slices white bread

1. Heat 1½oz (37gm) butter in a
saucepan and stir in flour. Cook
for 2 minutes.
2. Remove pan from heat and add
Madeira and stock. Season with
salt and pepper and cook,
stirring, until sauce thickens.
3. Add turkey, olives and lemon
juice and adjust seasoning.
4. Fry bread lightly in remaining
butter.
5. Cover each slice of fried bread
with a thick mound of turkey
mixture and serve very hot.

Cold dishes

There are all sorts of cold dishes in this chapter: salads and aspics, meat loaves and savoury jellies, snacks and pâtés.

JELLIED TOMATO SALAD
Serves 4

1½lb (¾ kilo) tomatoes, sieved
8oz (200gm) cheese, finely grated
salt and pepper
¼oz (6gm) gelatine
1 lettuce
watercress and celery curls to garnish

1. Mix the tomato and most of the cheese together. Season.
2. Dissolve the gelatine in 1 tablespoon hot water and mix into tomato mixture.
3. When it is beginning to set, stir well, pour into individual moulds and leave to set.
4. Break the lettuce into pieces and place on a dish. Turn out the tomato jellies on to it and garnish with rest of cheese, watercress and celery curls.

SALAD SANDWICH LOAF
Serves 4–6

1 uncut white sandwich loaf, preferably one day old
4oz (100gm) butter
¼ pint (125ml) bought mayonnaise
several different kinds of sandwich filling, e.g. chopped salad, chicken, shrimp, salmon, devilled egg, liver sausage, cheese
8oz (200gm) soft cream cheese
paprika pepper, radishes and chopped parsley to garnish

1. Slice the loaf horizontally, making seven or eight long slices about ¾ inch thick.
2. Remove all the crusts.
3. Spread each slice with the butter and mayonnaise.
4. Cover each with a different filling.
5. Stack the slices neatly, then cover the top and sides of the loaf with cream cheese.
6. Garnish with paprika pepper, radishes and parsley, and serve on a bed of lettuce.

SALAD CRUNCH
(Illustrated on page 71)
Serves 4

8oz (200gm) cooked potatoes
¼ small cabbage
2 red apples
juice of 1 lemon
2 tablespoons sweet and sour pickle
4oz (100gm) Wensleydale cheese
3 tablespoons salad cream
1 tomato

1. Dice the potatoes and mix with finely shredded cabbage in a salad bowl.
2. Wash but do not peel the apples and slice very thinly.
3. Dip in lemon juice and turn into the salad bowl, reserving a few slices for garnish.
4. Chop and add the pickle.
5. Cut the cheese into thin strips, add to salad bowl and toss all the ingredients gently in the salad cream.
6. Garnish with tomato and rest of apple slices.

SPROUT SALAD
Serves 4

12 Brussels sprouts
2oz (50gm) walnuts
1 dessert apple
1 celery heart
1 small onion
salt and pepper
2 tablespoons salad cream

1. Prepare the sprouts and shred
them finely.
2. Chop the walnuts and grate the
apple.
3. Chop the celery heart with the
onion.
4. Mix all ingredients together,
season to taste and add salad
cream.

WINTER SALAD
Serves 4

1 small firm cabbage
8oz (200gm) carrots
3oz (75gm) cheese, grated
2 tablespoons chopped chives
3oz (75gm) dates, chopped
2 tablespoons chopped parsley
1 carton natural yogurt
salt and pepper

1. Shred the cabbage finely.
2. Grate the carrots, then mix
with the remaining ingredients.
Season and pile in a bowl.

CHEESE, FRUIT AND NUT SALAD
Serves 4

8oz (200gm) curd cheese
1 tablespoon raisins
1 lettuce
6 canned peach halves
6 walnut halves
sliced cucumber and
watercress to garnish

1. Beat the cheese until smooth.
2. Put the raisins into boiling
water for 1–2 minutes to soften
them. Drain well and leave to
cool.
3. Mix with the cheese.
4. Place the lettuce leaves on a
dish, arrange the peach halves on
it, put a roughly heaped
tablespoon cheese mixture on
each and top with half a walnut.
5. Garnish with cucumber slices
and watercress sprigs.

FRENCH RICE SALAD
Serves 4

6oz (150gm) long-grain rice
¾ pint (375ml) water
¾ teaspoon salt
6oz (150gm) blue cheese,
crumbled
¼ pint (125ml) soured cream
1 tablespoon lemon juice
½ celery head, chopped finely
½ cucumber, cubed
1 bunch of radishes, sliced
1 bunch of chives, chopped
salt and pepper
4 tomatoes, sliced

1. Put rice, water and salt into a
saucepan.
2. Bring to the boil and stir once.
3. Lower heat to simmer. Cover
and cook for about 15 minutes, or
until rice is tender.
4. Mix together cheese, soured
cream and lemon juice in a bowl.
5. Mix together cooked rice,
celery, cucumber, radishes and
chives.
6. Season and add tomatoes.
7. Chill the salad, and garnish
with the cheese mixture before
serving.

PEARS WITH CREAM CHEESE
Serves 4

2 ripe pears
lemon juice
½oz (12gm) walnuts, chopped
8oz (200gm) cottage cheese
1 teaspoon chopped onion
salt and pepper
parsley to garnish

1. Peel pears, halve them and
remove cores.
2. Brush with lemon juice.
3. Stir walnuts into cottage
cheese, add onion and season.
4. Pile on to pear halves and
arrange on a serving dish.
5. Garnish with parsley and serve
with lettuce.

COTTAGE CHEESE AND ORANGE MOULD
Serves 4

2 tablespoons gelatine
¼ pint (125ml) cold water
1 large carton cottage cheese
¼ pint (125ml) soured cream
3 tablespoons honey
3 tablespoons orange juice
¼ teaspoon grated orange rind
½ level teaspoon salt
1 lettuce

1. Mix gelatine with cold water
in a small basin and dissolve over
a pan of hot water.
2. Meanwhile, combine cottage
cheese, soured cream, honey,
orange juice and rind and salt.
4. Add gelatine and stir until
blended.
5. Pour into mould, then chill
until firm.
6. Turn out on to a plate of
lettuce.

HAM AND CHICKEN MOUSSE
Serves 4

¼ pint (125ml) aspic jelly (see
Basic recipes, page 100)
1 hard-boiled egg, sliced
few peas
2 stuffed olives, sliced
4 mushrooms, sliced or
4 radishes, sliced
8oz (200gm) cooked chicken
2oz (50gm) cooked ham
2oz (50gm) mushrooms
¾ pint (375ml) milk
1oz (25gm) butter
1oz (25gm) flour
salt and pepper
½oz (12gm) gelatine
2 egg whites

1. Line a mould with aspic jelly.
2. Decorate with hard-boiled egg,
peas, olives, mushrooms or
radishes.
3. Cover with more aspic,
reserving a little, and allow to set
firmly in place.
4. Meanwhile, mince the chicken
and ham very finely.
5. Wash and cut up the
mushrooms and cook in some of
milk.
6. Strain the liquid, make it up to
½ pint (250ml) with the remaining
milk.
7. Melt butter in a saucepan. Add
flour, then remove from heat and
add milk, stirring well. Return to
heat and stir till sauce thickens.
8. Add minced chicken, ham and
remaining aspic to the sauce, and
season well.
9. Dissolve the gelatine in a little
water and add.
10. Whisk the egg whites until
stiff and fold in.
11. Pour into a mould and leave
to set.
12. Turn it out and serve with
lettuce.

HAM CORNETS
Serves 4

8oz (200gm) ham, thinly sliced
½ pint (250ml) aspic jelly (see
Basic recipes, page 100)
4oz (100gm) liver pâté or liver
sausage
4 tablespoons thick
mayonnaise

1. Trim any excess fat from the
ham.
2. Dip each slice into aspic and
curl it to fit inside a metal cornet
mould.
3. Fill with pâté and put in the
refrigerator to set.
4. Just before serving, ease ham
out of the metal cornet moulds
with a small knife and pipe in
mayonnaise.
5. Serve with salad.

AMSTERDAM SALAD
Serves 4

½ lettuce, finely shredded
3oz (75gm) boiled long-grain
rice (raw weight)
½ cucumber, chopped
1 small onion, cut into rings
8oz (200gm) ham, cut unto
strips
8oz (200gm) Gouda cheese,
cubed
1 can pimento, thinly sliced
1 small can button mushrooms

1. Place the lettuce in the base of
a salad bowl.
2. Combine all the other
ingredients together and mix
thoroughly.
3. Pile on top of the lettuce.
4. Serve with French dressing
separately (see Basic recipes,
page 100).

SUMMER HAM MOUSSE
Serves 4

1lb (½ kilo) ham
¼ pint (125ml) cream
1 egg white
½oz (12gm) gelatine
6 tablespoons water
salt and pepper
½ cucumber

1. Mince the ham twice, stir in
the cream and whisked egg white.
2. Dissolve the gelatine in water
and stir into the ham.
3. Season very well. Slice the
cucumber and line the sides of a
small mould or pudding basin.
4. Pour in the ham mixture and
leave to set.
5. Turn mousse out and serve
with salad.

ORANGE AND HAM ROLLS
Serves 4

1oz (25gm) butter
½ onion, grated
1 stick celery, finely chopped
2 tomatoes, skinned and
chopped
1oz (25gm) macaroni
grated rind and juice of
1 orange
1 teaspoon marjoram
salt and pepper
4 medium thick slices ham

1. Melt butter in a pan, add
onion, celery and tomatoes.
2. Fry gently for 5–10 minutes,
until tender.
3. Meanwhile, cook macaroni in
boiling, salted water for about 10
minutes or until tender.
4. Drain and mix with vegetables.
5. Add orange rind and juice,
marjoram and seasoning. Cook for
a further 5 minutes.
6. Trim ham slices, spread with
filling and roll up. Serve cold with
a salad.

POTTED HAM
Serves 4–6

2lb (1 kilo) lean bacon or ham
8oz (200gm) bacon or ham fat
¼ teaspoon pepper
¼ teaspoon nutmeg
pinch of cayenne pepper
a little clarified butter

1. Preheat oven to moderate, 350 deg F or gas 4 (180 deg C).
2. Mince the lean bacon or ham and bacon or ham fat twice or chop very finely. Mash well and liquidise or sieve.
3. Add the seasonings and mix very well.
4. Turn into a greased pie dish and cover with foil.
5. Bake in centre of oven for 45 minutes.
6. Spoon into small pots or jars and press down very firmly.
7. Brush with butter and serve cold with a mixed salad.

CRISPY BACON SALAD
(Illustrated on page 71)
Serves 4

Crisp little pieces of bacon incorporated in a salad.

4 streaky bacon rashers
2oz (50gm) Cheddar cheese
1 stick celery
2 hard-boiled eggs
2 tomatoes
1 lettuce
1 carton soured cream or
natural yogurt

1. Fry the bacon until it is crisp. Drain.
2. Cut the cheese into tiny squares and scrub and slice the celery.
3. Quarter the hard-boiled eggs.
4. Quarter the tomatoes and wash the lettuce.
5. Turn all the ingredients into separate small bowls and serve with a bowl of soured cream or yogurt.

SUMMER BEEF ROLL
Serves 4

1 packet sage and onion
stuffing
12oz (300gm) raw minced beef
4oz (100gm) streaky bacon,
de-rinded and minced
1 small onion, grated
1 teaspoon prepared mustard
salt and pepper
1 egg, beaten
breadcrumbs to coat

1. Preheat oven to moderately hot, 400 deg F or gas 6 (200 deg C).
2. Prepare stuffing as directed on packet.
3. Combine stuffing with minced beef, bacon, onion and mustard. Season.
4. Shape mixture into a roll, brush with egg and coat with breadcrumbs.
5. Place in a roasting tin and bake in centre of oven for 35–40 minutes, until golden.
6. Cut into slices and serve cold with salad.

BEEF LUNCHEON LOAF
Serves 4

1lb (½ kilo) lean beef steak
4oz (100gm) bacon, raw or
cooked
4oz (100gm) white breadcrumbs
1 teaspoon chopped parsley
good pinch of grated nutmeg
salt and pepper
½ teaspoon dried thyme
grated rind of 1 lemon
1 egg, beaten
4 tablespoons stock
¼ pint (125ml) aspic jelly (see
Basic recipes, page 100)

1. Mince the beef with the bacon; put into a bowl.
2. Stir in the breadcrumbs, parsley and nutmeg.
3. Season well with salt and pepper and add thyme and lemon rind.
4. Bind mixture together with egg and stock.
5. Form into a roll and tie very securely in a clean teatowel.
6. Put into a pan of boiling water and simmer for 2½ hours.
7. Remove from the pan and tighten the cloth.
8. Leave overnight pressed between two weights.
9. Untie the cloth and pour aspic jelly over loaf.
10. Leave to set. Slice to serve.

COLD STUFFED BREAST OF LAMB
Serves 4–6

4oz (100gm) long-grain rice
½ pint (250ml) stock or water
1 teaspoon salt
pinch of mixed herbs
freshly chopped mint
grated rind of 1 lemon
salt and pepper
1 egg, beaten
1 large breast of lamb
1oz (25gm) lard

1. Preheat oven to moderate to moderately hot, 375 deg F or gas 5 (190 deg C).
2. Place rice, stock or water and salt in a saucepan and bring to the boil. Stir once.
3. Lower heat to simmer, cover with a tightly fitting lid and simmer for 15 minutes.
4. Turn into a basin and leave to cool. Mix in herbs, mint, lemon rind and seasoning.
5. Bind with egg and spread over lamb.
6. Roll up and tie securely.
7. Place in a baking tin with fat and bake in centre of oven for 40–50 minutes.
8. Leave until cold, slice and serve accompanied by a salad.

JELLIED LAMB SLICES
(Illustrated on page 71)
Serves 4

½oz (12gm) gelatine
¾ pint (375ml) rich meat stock
juice of ½ lemon
salt and pepper
8 thin slices cold lamb
2 hard-boiled eggs
3 young cooked carrots
2oz (50gm) cooked fresh peas

1. Put the gelatine into the stock.
2. Stir over a very low heat until dissolved.
3. Add the lemon juice and leave to get cold but do not allow to set.
4. Arrange the lamb in a dish and slice the eggs and the carrots and put over the meat.
5. Scatter the peas over the lamb, then pour the jelly over. Leave to set.
6. Serve with a green salad.

LIVER PATE
Serves 4–6

12oz (300gm) pork fat
1lb (½ kilo) calf's liver
4oz (100gm) pie veal
1 small onion
8 anchovy fillets
4oz (100gm) plain flour
3 eggs
½ pint (250ml) milk
2 teaspoons salt
½ teaspoon pepper

1. Preheat oven to very moderate, 325 deg F or gas 3 (170 deg C).
2. Line a casserole with thin slices of a good half of pork fat.
3. Cut up the liver, veal, rest of fat, onion and anchovies and mince three times.
4. Sift flour into a bowl. Add eggs. Gradually beat in half the milk until batter is smooth. Add rest of milk.
5. Slowly stir in the liver mixture and season well.
6. Put mixture in the casserole, cover and stand it in a tin containing a little water.
7. Cook in centre of oven for 1½ hours. Serve cold and sliced.

PORK CHOPS IN LEMON ASPIC
Serves 4

2 pig's trotters, split in half by butcher
4 lean pork chops
1 tablespoon lemon juice
1 bayleaf
3 cloves
salt and pepper

1. Wash pig's trotters.
2. Trim the fat from 4 pork chops and cover with water in a pan with the trotters.
3. Add lemon juice, bayleaf, cloves, salt and pepper.
4. Bring to the boil and simmer for 1 hour. Skim well.
5. Arrange the chops in a shallow dish with the meat from the cooked trotters.
6. Reduce the stock until just sufficient to cover the chops.
7. Pour over and leave to set.
8. Serve with a salad.

PORK AND PEARS
Serves 4

Cold pork chops with a pear dressing.

3 tablespoons white wine vinegar
2 teaspoons English mustard
salt and pepper
3 tablespoons olive oil
1 bunch watercress
2 pears
4 pork chops, cooked and chilled

1. Blend vinegar, mustard and seasoning together in a bowl.
2. Gradually beat in the oil, drop by drop.
3. Wash and chop watercress, then add to mixture.
4. Peel, core and slice pears.
5. Toss in oil and watercress mixture.
6. Serve over the cold pork chops.

CELERY AND CHICKEN SALAD
Serves 4

1 cooked chicken (3lb or 1½ kilo)
2 sticks celery
1 green pepper
1 teaspoon grated onion
¼ pint (125ml) mayonnaise
¼ pint (125ml) single cream
1 teaspoon lemon juice
salt and pepper
1 lettuce
pineapple chunks and
asparagus to garnish

1. Cut the chicken into pieces, chop the celery and mince the pepper.
2. Mix these ingredients with the onion, mayonnaise, cream and lemon juice and season well.
3. Pile on to a bed of lettuce leaves and surround with pineapple and asparagus.

CHICKEN MOULD
Serves 4

1 chicken (3lb or 1½ kilo)
2oz (50gm) gelatine
¼ pint (125ml) water
¾ pint (375ml) chicken stock
1 tablespoon cooked peas
1 tablespoon chopped red pepper
1 tomato, sliced
1 hard-boiled egg, sliced

1. Cook the chicken and remove the meat from the bones.
2. Dissolve the gelatine in the water and add to the hot stock.
3. When the jelly is beginning to set, fold in the pieces of chicken, the peas and red pepper.
4. Turn into a mould to set.
5. When firm, turn out and serve cut in slices, garnished with tomato and egg.

CHICKEN AND BACON PATE
Serves 4

1oz (25gm) butter
4oz (100gm) pig's liver, sliced
4oz (100gm) gammon or bacon, cooked and chopped
4oz (100gm) cold, cooked chicken
1 garlic clove
1 tablespoon brandy or sherry
3 tablespoons double cream
salt and pepper
1oz (25gm) butter, melted

1. Melt the butter and fry the liver and gammon or bacon gently for 10 minutes.
2. Remove from the pan and mince finely together with the chicken and garlic.
3. Stir in the brandy or sherry and cream and season to taste.
4. Turn the mixture into a small, earthenware dish. Smooth the top, pour melted butter over and leave to set.
5. Serve chilled with hot toast.

CHICKEN AND MUSHROOM MOULD
Serves 4

½ pint (250ml) aspic jelly (see Basic recipes, page 100)
½ cucumber
4oz (100gm) mushrooms
a little milk
¼ pint (125ml) white sauce (see Basic recipes, page 100)
8oz (200gm) cooked chicken
salt and pepper

1. Pour a little aspic into four moulds, decorate with cubed cucumber and allow to set.
2. Chop and cook mushrooms in a little milk.
3. Mix them with the remaining aspic, white sauce and chopped chicken.
4. Season well, then pour into the moulds.
5. Leave to set, then turn out on to a bed of mixed salad.

CHICKEN AND RICE SALAD
Serves 4

8oz (200gm) long-grain rice
1 garlic clove (optional)
4 tablespoons salad oil
1–2 tablespoons wine or tarragon vinegar
salt and pepper
1 heaped tablespoon currants
1 green pepper
2 large tomatoes
12oz (300gm) cooked chicken

1. Cook the rice in plenty of fast-boiling, salted water until just tender, then drain very thoroughly.
2. Meanwhile, rub a salad bowl with the cut garlic clove, if used, and add oil, vinegar and seasoning, mixing well.
3. Add the hot rice and currants and mix thoroughly with the dressing.
4. De-seed and slice the green pepper very finely.
5. Skin, de-seed and chop the tomato and cut the chicken into bite-size pieces.
6. Stir pepper, tomato and chicken into the salad, reserving a few pieces of pepper and tomato for sprinkling over the top of the salad.
7. Cover and set aside in a cool place for 1 hour, for the flavours to blend.

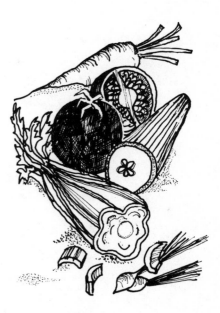

COLD CHICKEN SALAD AND CHERRIES
(Illustrated on page 71)
Serves 4–6

1 cold roasted chicken (3lb or 1½ kilo)
1lb (½ kilo) fresh or canned red cherries
4 tablespoons red wine
2oz (50gm) lump sugar
grated rind and juice of 1 orange
1 tablespoon redcurrant jelly

1. Joint and slice the chicken; put on to a flat dish.
2. Stone all the cherries. Put wine, sugar and orange rind and juice into a pan.
3. Bring up to the boil and add the cherries.
4. Cook very slowly for about 5 minutes, until fruit is tender.
5. Stir in the redcurrant jelly. When melted, pour over the chicken.
6. Chill well and serve surrounded with lettuce leaves and accompanied with a side salad of sliced tomatoes.

ICE COLD CHICKEN SOUFFLES
Serves 4

½oz (12gm) gelatine
½ pint (250ml) aspic jelly (see Basic recipes, page 100)
½ pint (250ml) white sauce (see Basic recipes, page 100)
8oz (200gm) cooked chicken, minced
salt and pepper
1 small can evaporated milk or ¼ pint (125ml) double cream
2 egg whites
radishes and cucumber to garnish

1. Tie some greaseproof paper firmly round the outsides of four individual dishes so the paper stands proud.
2. Dissolve the gelatine slowly in the liquid aspic jelly.
3. Mix with the white sauce and chicken. Season and leave until nearly set.
4. Whip the evaporated milk or double cream stiffly and fold it into the mixture.
5. Add the stiffly beaten egg whites.
6. Pour quickly into the soufflé dishes and leave in a cold place to set.
7. When firm, remove the papers carefully and garnish with radishes and cucumber.

MUSHROOM, GREEN PEPPER AND CHICORY SALAD
Serves 4

8oz (200gm) cooked chicken, shredded
8oz (200gm) button mushrooms
1 green pepper
1 large or 2 small chicory heads
¼ pint (125ml) French dressing (see Basic recipes, page 100)

1. Put the chicken into a bowl. Wash, slice and add the mushrooms.
2. De-seed the pepper and cut into very thin slices.
3. Chop chicory (reserving 8 large leaves) and toss with the mushrooms and pepper in French dressing.
4. Serve piled on chicory leaves arranged like a star.

VIRGINIA CHICKEN SALAD
Serves 3–4

2 medium dessert apples
3 tablespoons lemon juice
⅛ pint (63ml) double cream
2 tablespoons salad cream
¼ teaspoon salt
8oz (200gm) cooked chicken, diced
4 sticks celery, sliced
1 tablespoon walnuts, chopped
lettuce leaves
1 small, red apple

1. Peel and core the dessert apples.
2. Cut into small dice and toss with 1 tablespoon lemon juice.
3. Lightly whip the cream and stir into it the salad cream, salt and 1 tablespoon lemon juice.
4. Add the diced apple, chicken, celery and nuts, mix gently and set aside in a cool place.
5. Arrange the lettuce leaves around a flat dish and pile the chicken salad in the centre. Cut the unpeeled red apple into slices, dip in the remaining lemon juice and use to garnish the salad.

SEAFOOD MOULDS
Serves 4

1lb (½ kilo) cooked white fish
2 tablespoons water
½oz (12gm) gelatine
¾ pint (375ml) tomato juice
1 teaspoon salad cream
watercress and radishes to garnish

1. Flake the fish, removing the skin and bones.
2. Put the water and gelatine into a basin and dissolve over a pan of hot water. Remove basin from pan.
3. Add the tomato juice, salad cream and fish.
4. Pour into wetted fish-shaped moulds or other small moulds.
5. When set, turn out and garnish with watercress and radishes. Serve with salad.

PRAWN AND EGG MOULD
Serves 4

2 packets frozen prawns
1 small packet frozen peas
1 pint (approximately ½ litre)
aspic jelly (see Basic recipes,
page 100)
3 hard-boiled eggs

1. Thaw the prawns and cook the
peas in boiling, salted water.
2. Pour a little aspic into a mould,
then set a few prawns in it.
3. When this is set, mix the
remaining prawns, quartered
eggs, and peas with rest of aspic
and pour into the mould.
4. Turn out when set, chill in the
refrigerator and serve with salad.

SHRIMP AND EGG FLAN
Serves 4

shortcrust pastry made with
4oz (100gm) flour (see Basic
recipes, page 100)
4oz (100gm) shelled prawns or
shrimps
¼ pint (125ml) white sauce (see
Basic recipes, page 100)
2 eggs
1oz (25gm) butter
½ cucumber
1–2 tomatoes

1. Preheat oven to moderately
hot, 400 deg F or gas 6 (200 deg C).
2. Roll out the pastry and line a
7-inch (18cm) flan case.
3. Prick the base and line with
greaseproof paper. Fill with
baking beans.
4. Bake for 10 minutes on the
centre shelf, remove beans and
paper and cook for a further 5
minutes.
5. Mix the prawns with the white
sauce.
6. Scramble the eggs in butter.
7. Peel and slice the cucumber;
skin and slice the tomatoes.
8. Mark the flan case into
sections and put in alternate
portions of shrimp and egg,
dividing them with slices of
cucumber.
9. Arrange tomato slices in the
centre.

LEEK AND SHRIMP SALAD
Serves 4

4 young leeks
6 tablespoons olive oil
3 tablespoons white wine
vinegar
salt and pepper
2 tablespoons cream
¼ pint (125ml) picked shrimps
paprika pepper

1. Wash and trim the leeks and
blanch in boiling, salted water for
5–6 minutes. Lift out, drain and
chill well.
2. Mix together oil, vinegar and
seasoning. Add the cream and
whisk again.
3. Toss leeks in this mixture with
the picked shrimps.
4. Serve chilled and scattered
with paprika pepper and
watercress.

SALMON MAYONNAISE
Serves 4

½ cucumber, finely sliced
1 lettuce
4 tablespoons French dressing
(see Basic recipes, page 100)
8oz (200gm) salmon, fresh or
canned
mayonnaise
sprigs of parsley
3 tomatoes, sliced
3oz (75gm) cooked peas

1. Toss the cucumber and lettuce
in the French dressing.
2. Arrange on a dish, with the
cold cooked salmon on top.
3. Coat the salmon with
mayonnaise.
4. Garnish with parsley, tomatoes
and cooked peas.

GOLDEN EGGS
Serves 2

4 hard-boiled eggs
1 small can salmon
3 gherkins
2 teaspoons vinegar
salt and pepper
4 tablespoons salad cream
2 tablespoons chopped parsley
1 tablespoon top of the milk
watercress or lettuce

1. Cut the eggs in half lengthways
and remove the yolk.
2. Remove skin and bone from the
salmon.
3. Chop the gherkins and 2 egg
yolks.
4. Mix the salmon, gherkins and
chopped egg yolks with the
vinegar and seasoning. Pile the
mixture into the egg whites.
5. Combine the salad cream and
parsley with enough milk to give
a coating consistency.
6. Place the stuffed eggs on a bed
of watercress or lettuce. Pour the
dressing over.
7. Sieve the remaining 2 egg
yolks and sprinkle over the
stuffed eggs.
8. Serve with salad.

TUNA SALAD
Serves 4

1 large can tuna fish
1 small head celery
cooked carrot rings
cocktail onions
4 tablespoons salad cream
tomato slices to garnish

1. Cut the tuna into cubes.
2. Slice the celery thinly.
3. Mix all the ingredients together and stir in salad cream.
4. Serve surrounded with sliced tomato.

STUFFED AVOCADO PEARS
Serves 4

2 avocado pears
2 red apples
4 sticks celery
2 teaspoons finely chopped onion
4oz (100gm) crab or lobster
2 teaspoons chopped parsley
2 tablespoons French dressing (see Basic recipes, page 100)

1. Cut avocado pears in half and remove stones.
2. Core apples and dice them.
3. Mix apple and celery together with the onion, crab or lobster and parsley.
4. Add the French dressing.
5. Spoon on to each half of avocado pear.
6. Serve with extra French dressing.

CRAB MOUSSE
Serves 4

8oz (200gm) crab meat
1½oz (37gm) butter
4 tablespoons white sauce (see Basic recipes, page 100)
salt
cayenne pepper
1 tablespoon dry sherry
1 teaspoon lemon juice
scant ½ pint (250ml) aspic jelly (see Basic recipes, page 100)
4 tablespoons cream, lightly whipped
2 egg whites
parsley sprigs to garnish

1. Pound the crab meat until smooth in a mortar or put it into an electric liquidiser.
2. Beat the butter until soft and creamy and mix into the crab meat with the white sauce.
3. Season very well with salt and cayenne pepper.
4. Mix in the sherry, lemon juice, aspic jelly and cream.
5. Put into a cold place to cool but do not allow to set.
6. Whisk the egg whites stiffly and fold into the mixture.
7. Turn into a glass bowl and leave to set firmly.
8. Garnish with a ring of parsley sprigs, and serve with a bowl of green salad and a tomato salad.

WHITE FISH SALAD
Serves 4

1 lettuce
8oz (200gm) cooked cod or other white fish
1 tablespoon peas
1 tablespoon chopped cauliflower
1 tablespoon chopped gherkins
2 tomatoes, chopped
¼ pint (125ml) mayonnaise

1. Arrange the lettuce round the edge of a dish.
2. Mix all the other ingredients together and place in the centre.

FISH TERRINE
Serves 6

8oz (200gm) turbot or halibut
3oz (75gm) butter
4oz (100gm) fresh, white breadcrumbs
½ tablespoon chopped parsley
salt and cayenne pepper
pinch of ground mace
1 egg yolk, beaten
4 tablespoons milk
8oz (200gm) haddock

1. Preheat oven to very moderate, 325 deg F or gas 3 (170 deg C).
2. Clean and chop up the turbot or halibut and mix with half the butter.
3. Add the breadcrumbs and parsley and season well.
4. Add mace and bind together with egg and milk.
5. Skin and bone haddock and cut into thin strips.
6. Layer turbot mixture and haddock strips into a small casserole dish, seasoning each layer well.
7. Put dabs of butter on top.
8. Cover and cook in a roasting tin of cold water in centre of oven for 3 hours.
9. Do not uncover until cold. Serve chilled, with a crisp salad.

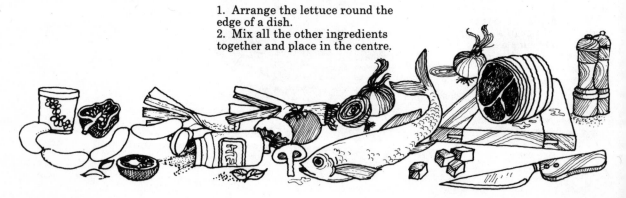

POTATO AND SARDINE SALAD
Serves 4

3 large new potatoes
1 small onion
salt and pepper
4 tablespoons French dressing
(see Basic recipes, page 100)
2 cans sardines
juice of 1 lemon
chopped parsley
1 carrot, grated
1 lettuce

1. Cook the potatoes. When cold, cut into cubes and chop the onion finely. Mix the two ingredients together.
2. Add seasoning and toss the mixture in French dressing.
3. Pile in the centre of a dish.
4. Arrange the sardines round and sprinkle with lemon juice and parsley. Serve with carrot and lettuce leaves.

SARDINE AND BEETROOT SALAD
Serves 4

2 large cans sardines
2 eating apples
1 medium cooked beetroot
4–6 tablespoons mayonnaise
lettuce and apple slices to garnish

1. Mash sardines in a bowl.
2. Grate apples and beetroot and mix with sardines.
3. Add mayonnaise to moisten.
4. Garnish with lettuce and sliced apple.

SALAD SARDINIA
Serves 4

3oz (75gm) boiled long-grain rice (raw weight)
1 green pepper, cut into wedges and blanched
4 tomatoes, cut into 8 and seeded
1 stick celery, sliced
2 cans sardines, drained
6 tablespoons olive oil
2 tablespoons lemon juice
salt
freshly ground black pepper
1 tablespoon chopped parsley

1. Mix together rice, pepper, tomatoes, celery and sardines, keeping the sardines whole.
2. In a separate bowl whisk rest of ingredients together and pour over the salad.
3. Mix in lightly and serve.

MOULDED SALMON SALAD
Serves 4

¼ pint (125ml) salad cream
¼ pint (125ml) milk
½oz (12gm) gelatine
⅛ pint (63ml) warm water
8oz (200gm) salmon, flaked
1 lettuce
½ cucumber, sliced

1. Mix salad cream and milk together and warm slightly in a saucepan.
2. Add gelatine dissolved in the warm water.
3. Stir for a few moments, then fold in the fish.
4. Turn into a mould and leave to set.
5. When quite firm turn out and serve with crisp lettuce and slices of cucumber.

FISH MOUSSE
Serves 4

8oz (200gm) cooked white fish
pepper
3 tablespoons lemon juice
¼ pint (125ml) salad cream
½ teaspoon celery salt
¾oz (18gm) gelatine
scant ½ pint (250ml) fish stock
¼ pint (125ml) evaporated milk

1. Mix the fish, pepper, lemon juice, salad cream and celery salt together.
2. Dissolve the gelatine in the stock and allow to cool before adding it to the fish.
3. Whisk the evaporated milk and add to fish when it is almost setting.
4. When set, turn out and serve with salad.

SWEET AND SOUR MACKEREL
Serves 4

4 mackerel
1 carrot
1 onion
2 sugar lumps
2 bayleaves
salt and peppercorns
1 teaspoon vinegar
1 lettuce
tomato and cucumber slices

1. Clean the mackerel and cut off the heads and tails. Cut fish into eight pieces.
2. Put the pieces in a saucepan and cover with water.
3. Add sliced carrot and onion, sugar, bayleaves, salt, a few peppercorns and vinegar.
4. Simmer gently for 30 minutes, then strain.
5. Chill, then serve on a bed of lettuce with tomato and cucumber slices.

Vegetable dishes

As there's such a wide variety of vegetables available throughout the year, it is possible to make them into some of the most exciting dishes you can serve.

BEAN SUPPER
Serves 4

8oz (200gm) streaky bacon
2 medium cans baked beans
1 hard-boiled egg, quartered
4 slices bread, toasted and cut into triangles

1. Curl up bacon into rolls and place on skewers.
2. Grill until cooked, then remove from the skewers.
3. Heat the baked beans and arrange on a serving dish.
4. Garnish with bacon rolls and egg.
5. Place toast round the edge of the serving dish.

CHEESE-CAPPED BROAD BEANS
Serves 4

1 medium can broad beans
1 packet (½ pint or 250ml) onion sauce mix
¼ pint (125ml) milk
2oz (50gm) cheese, grated

1. Heat beans in their own liquid. Drain them and reserve liquid.
2. Make onion sauce following directions on the packet, using 4 tablespoons of bean liquid and the milk. Cook for 1 minute.
3. Return beans to the sauce, and heat through well.
4. Pour into a flameproof dish.
5. Sprinkle with cheese and grill until brown.

BROCCOLI UNDER COVER
Serves 4

1 large packet frozen broccoli
1 packet (½ pint or 250ml) cheese sauce mix (or see Basic recipes, page 100)
½ pint (250ml) milk
4 eggs, separated
1oz (25gm) cheese, grated

1. Cook broccoli as directed on packet.
2. Make up sauce with the milk, as directed on the packet.
3. Whisk egg whites and fold gently into cheese sauce.
4. Drain broccoli and place in a hot ovenware dish.
5. Spoon sauce over broccoli.
6. Make four hollows in cheese mixture and drop an egg yolk into each.
7. Sprinkle with cheese and grill until cheese is brown and eggs are cooked.

STUFFED CABBAGE LEAVES
Serves 4

1oz (25gm) butter
1 onion, finely chopped
1lb (½ kilo) minced meat
3 tomatoes, skinned
2 teaspoons chopped parsley
2 tablespoons cooked rice
salt and pepper
12 cabbage leaves
¼–½ pint (125–250ml) stock

1. Preheat oven to moderate, 350 deg F or gas 4 (180 deg C).
2. Melt the butter and fry the onion, meat and sliced tomatoes for 5–10 minutes.
3. Add parsley, rice and seasoning and cook for a further 3–4 minutes.
4. Meanwhile, blanch the cabbage leaves by dipping into boiling water for 2 minutes, then drain.
5. Put a spoonful of filling in each leaf and roll up, tucking the ends in to form a neat package.
6. Arrange in an ovenware dish and pour the stock over.
7. Cover and cook in centre of oven for 45 minutes.
8. Arrange the leaves on a dish and serve with rice and a tomato sauce.

CABBAGE SURPRISE
Serves 4

12 large cabbage leaves
8oz (200gm) ham, chopped
6oz (150gm) white breadcrumbs
3oz (75gm) suet, shredded
1 egg, beaten
salt and pepper
1 teaspoon dried herbs
1 pint (approximately ½ litre)
meat stock

1. Preheat oven to moderately hot, 400 deg F or gas 6 (200 deg C).
2. Put the cabbage leaves in boiling water for 2 minutes until softened. Drain well.
3. Mix together the ham, breadcrumbs and suet.
4. Bind with the egg and season well. Add herbs and spoon on to the cabbage leaves.
5. Fold them up enclosing the stuffing and tie each with string.
6. Arrange in a baking dish, add the stock and cover.
7. Cook in centre of oven for 40 minutes.

CARROT SOUFFLE
Serves 4

1½lb (¾ kilo) carrots
3oz (75gm) butter
3oz (75gm) flour
½ pint (250ml) milk
salt and pepper
1 tablespoon grated onion
1 tablespoon chopped parsley
3 eggs, separated

1. Preheat oven to moderate, 350 deg F or gas 4 (180 deg C).
2. Put scrubbed carrots into boiling, salted water and cook until really tender.
3. Drain well and mash finely.
4. Prepare a sauce by melting the butter in a saucepan and mixing in the flour. Cook for a few minutes, remove from the heat and blend in the milk.
5. Season and, stirring, bring to the boil. Simmer for 3 minutes.
6. Stir in the carrots, onion and parsley.
7. Remove from the heat and stir in the egg yolks.
8. Whisk the whites stiffly and fold into the mixture.
9. Turn into a buttered baking dish.
10. Bake in centre of oven for 25 minutes.
11. Serve, at once, with a fresh salad.

CAULIFLOWER CHEESE
(Illustrated on page 72)
Serves 4

1 cauliflower
2oz (50gm) butter
2oz (50gm) flour
1 pint (approximately ½ litre)
milk
salt and pepper
4oz (100gm) cheese, grated
8 bacon rashers

1. Wash cauliflower and break into sprigs.
2. Put in a pan with a little salted, boiling water.
3. Cook for 10 minutes until tender.
4. Drain and put cauliflower in a pie dish.
5. Melt butter in a saucepan, mix in flour, beat in milk and season well.
6. Cook, stirring, until mixture thickens.
7. Add 2½oz (62gm) cheese.
8. Pour sauce over the cauliflower and sprinkle with the rest of the cheese.
9. Grill until brown.
10. Roll up each bacon rasher and grill until crisp. Arrange round cauliflower and serve immediately.

SCRAMBLE OF CELERY
Serves 4

1 can condensed celery soup
8 eggs
4 slices hot buttered toast

1. Heat undiluted soup in a saucepan.
2. Beat the eggs together lightly and pour into the soup.
3. Stir over a medium heat until just set.
4. Serve at once on hot buttered toast.

CELERY, LEEK AND CHEESE PIE
Serves 4

3 leeks
3 sticks celery
¾ pint (375ml) milk
salt and pepper
¾oz (18gm) butter
1oz (25gm) flour
4oz (100gm) cheese, grated
4oz (100gm) macaroni
fresh breadcrumbs

1. Cut the leeks and celery into pieces.
2. Wash them carefully.
3. Place them in a pan with the milk, season and cook for about 30 minutes, until the vegetables are tender.
4. Strain off the liquor and reserve it.
5. Melt the butter in a saucepan and add the flour. Remove from heat and beat in the strained liquor to make a sauce. Add the cheese.
6. Cook the macaroni in boiling, salted water for about 10 minutes until tender.
7. Place it in a buttered pie dish and cover with the leeks and celery.
8. Pour the sauce over, then sprinkle with a few fresh breadcrumbs and brown under the grill.

CHILLI CON CARNE
Serves 4

12oz (300gm) long-grain rice
1½ pints (approximately ¾ litre)
water
1½ teaspoons salt
1¼lb (just under ¾ kilo) minced
beef
½ garlic clove, chopped
3 tablespoons oil
salt and chilli powder to taste
1lb (½ kilo) tomatoes, fresh or
canned
1½ pints (approximately ¾ litre)
stock
1 medium can red kidney
beans, drained, or baked beans

1. Put rice, water and salt in a
saucepan.
2. Bring to the boil and stir once.
3. Lower heat to simmer.
4. Cover tightly and cook for 15
minutes, until rice is tender and
liquid absorbed.
5. Fry meat and garlic in oil.
6. Salt and spice heavily with
chilli powder.
7. Add tomatoes and then stock.
8. Cook for 10 minutes, then mix
in the beans and let them heat
through.
9. Spoon over hot, cooked rice
and serve at once.

MUSHROOM FLAN
Serves 4

shortcrust pastry made with
4oz (100gm) flour (see Basic
recipes, page 100)
1 small onion
2oz (50gm) butter
½ pint (250ml) milk
salt and pepper
1 bayleaf
2 blades mace
1½oz (31gm) flour
4oz (100gm) button mushrooms
1 egg, separated
2 tablespoons cream

1. Preheat oven to moderately
hot, 400 deg F or gas 6 (200 deg C).
2. Roll out pastry and line a
6-inch (15cm) flan ring or
sandwich cake tin. Reserve the
pastry trimmings.
3. Skin the onion, slice and chop
finely. Melt 1½oz (37gm) butter
and cook onion until tender but
not brown.
4. Season milk with salt and
pepper then add bayleaf and mace,
and bring to the boil.
5. Blend flour into the onion, then
add strained milk.
6. Return to pan and cook,
stirring, until mixture thickens.
7. Quarter mushrooms and cook
in rest of butter.
8. Stir into sauce with egg yolk
and cream. Pour into flan case.
9. Make a lattice work top with
pastry trimmings. Brush with egg
white and bake in centre of oven
for 25 minutes.

MONDAY MARROW CASSEROLE
Serves 4

1 small marrow
salt and pepper
8oz (200gm) cooked cold meat,
minced or finely chopped
1 packet (1 pint or
approximately ½ litre) tomato
soup
¾ pint (375ml) water
1–2 teaspoons Worcestershire
sauce
1–2 teaspoons malt vinegar

1. Preheat oven to hot, 425 deg F
or gas 7 (220 deg C).
2. Slice the marrow into seven or
eight rings each 1 inch thick.
3. Scoop out and discard the
seeds, skin and arrange in a
shallow ovenware dish.
4. Season the cooked meat and
use to fill the centre of each ring.
5. Make the soup as directed on
the packet but using ¾ pint (375ml)
water only.
6. Stir in the Worcestershire
sauce and vinegar then pour over
the marrow rings.
7. Bake in centre of oven for
30–40 minutes.

MUSHROOM PANCAKE LAYER
Serves 4

½ pint (250ml) pancake batter
(see Basic recipes, page 100)
8oz (200gm) mushrooms
3oz (75gm) butter
salt and pepper
grated nutmeg
4 tablespoons double cream

1. Pour a little batter into a
small, greased frying pan. Cook
each pancake until golden on
both sides. Keep them hot.
2. Thinly slice the mushrooms.
3. Cook in butter with salt,
pepper and nutmeg.
4. Add cream.
5. Spread mixture on to pancakes,
then pile one on top of the other.
6. Cut pancake layer as you
would cut a cake and serve with
fried eggs cooked in butter.

SPINACH AND PASTA PIE
Serves 4

1lb (½ kilo) small pasta shapes
2lb (1 kilo) spinach
1oz (25gm) butter
3 tablespoons oil
12oz (300gm) mushrooms
1 garlic clove
salt and pepper
2oz (50gm) Parmesan cheese

1. Preheat oven to moderately hot, 400 deg F or gas 6 (200 deg C).
2. Boil pasta in salted water until almost tender, then drain thoroughly.
3. Prepare and cook spinach. Drain well and stir in the butter.
4. Heat oil in a pan, add chopped mushrooms, crushed garlic, salt and pepper. Simmer for 2 minutes.
5. Grease an ovenproof dish and arrange layers of spinach, pasta, cheese and mushrooms until the dish is full, reserving a little cheese to sprinkle over the top.
6. Bake in centre of oven for about 10 minutes.

ONION CRISP
Serves 4

12 small onions
½ pint (250ml) milk
a little water
4 tablespoons cooked peas
1oz (25gm) butter
1oz (25gm) flour
salt and pepper
crushed potato crisps
salted peanuts

1. Preheat oven to hot, 425 deg F or gas 7 (220 deg C).
2. Skin the onions and cook in milk and a little water until tender.
3. Remove them whole and put into a greased dish with the peas.
4. Melt the butter and add the flour.
5. Blend in half the milk and water in which the onions were cooked.
6. Heat gently, stirring, until it thickens. Season well.
7. Pour sauce over the onions and sprinkle thickly with crisps and chopped salted peanuts.
8. Reheat in the oven for a few minutes, then serve with pork sausages.

FRENCH ONION SOUP
(Illustrated on page 72)
Serves 3–4

Here's a really good soup that is a meal in itself for a chilly night.

1lb (½ kilo) onions
1oz (25gm) butter
1¾ pints (1 scant litre) stock
salt and pepper
1oz (25gm) flour
small slices French bread, toasted
Parmesan cheese, grated

1. Skin and slice the onions very thinly.
2. Melt the butter in a pan and add the onions.
3. Cover with a well fitting lid and cook very slowly for about 20 minutes, stirring occasionally, or until the onions are tender but not brown.
4. Add 1½ pints (approximately ¾ litre) stock to the onions.
5. Season, stir and allow to heat through. Simmer for 30 minutes.
6. Blend the flour with the remaining stock and stir into the soup.
7. Reheat and cook for 10 minutes.
8. Serve in a tureen with the toasted French bread floating on top. Sprinkle with cheese.

RICE-STUFFED GREEN PEPPERS
(Illustrated on page 72)
Serves 4

4 medium green peppers
1oz (25gm) butter
1 small onion, finely chopped
4oz (100gm) minced beef
1 teaspoon chopped parsley
1 can (8oz or 200gm) tomatoes
1 egg
2oz (50gm) cooked long-grain rice (raw weight)
salt and pepper

1. Preheat oven to moderate, 350 deg F or gas 4 (180 deg C).
2. Cut peppers in half and scoop out seeds.
3. Plunge them into boiling water for 5 minutes. Drain them and arrange in a buttered baking dish.
4. To prepare the stuffing, melt the butter and fry onion gently until tender.
5. Add minced beef and cook until brown.
6. Take pan off heat and stir in parsley, tomatoes and egg.
7. Add rice, season well and spoon filling into pepper shells.
8. Place on a baking tray in centre of oven for 45 minutes. Serve with tomato sauce.

BAKED POTATO CAKE
Serves 4

4 medium old potatoes
2 pickled herrings
6oz (150gm) salami
1 can (6oz or 150gm) cream
1 teaspoon lemon juice
pepper
4oz (100gm) breadcrumbs
2oz (50gm) butter

1. Preheat oven to hot, 425 deg F or gas 7 (220 deg C).
2. Scrub the potatoes, prick with a fork and bake in oven for 45 minutes. Turn oven down to moderately hot, 400 deg F or gas 6 (200 deg C).
3. Remove the skins and cut the potatoes into thin slices.
4. Chop the herrings and slice the salami.
5. Mix the cream with the lemon juice.
6. Butter an ovenware dish and fill it with alternate layers of potato, herring and salami, starting and finishing with a layer of potatoes. Spread each layer with cream and season with pepper.
7. Cover the top with breadcrumbs and dot with butter.
8. Bake in centre of oven for 40 minutes.
9. Remove from the oven and serve immediately.

POTATO NUT CAKES
Serves 4

4oz (100gm) ground walnuts
12oz (300gm) mashed potato
1 onion, chopped and fried
1 egg
2 tablespoons minced parsley
½ teaspoon dried sage
4oz (100gm) breadcrumbs
salt and pepper
1 egg, beaten
breadcrumbs for coating
fat for frying

1. Mix together walnuts, potato, onion, egg, parsley, sage, breadcrumbs, salt and pepper.
2. Form into rissoles, coat in egg and breadcrumbs and fry in hot fat. Drain on absorbent paper.
3. Serve hot, with vegetables and gravy, or cold with salad.

POTATO OMELETTE
Serves 4

2 medium potatoes, cooked and diced
2oz (50gm) butter
1 teaspoon chopped onion
salt and pepper
8 eggs

1. Fry the potato in melted butter with the onion, until just lightly browned.
2. Pour the seasoned, beaten eggs over.
3. Stir lightly with a palette knife and leave to set and brown lightly.
4. Slide on to a plate and divide into four to serve.

SCALLOPED POTATOES
Serves 4

1lb (½ kilo) potatoes
1oz (25gm) butter
3 level tablespoons flour
salt and pepper
¾ pint (375ml) milk
4oz (100gm) Cheddar cheese, grated
4oz (100gm) bacon, rinded and chopped
2 hard-boiled eggs, sliced
½oz (12gm) fresh white breadcrumbs

1. Preheat oven to hot, 425 deg F or gas 7 (220 deg C).
2. Cook potatoes in boiling, salted water until tender, then drain and slice thickly.
3. Melt butter and stir in flour, salt and pepper. Cook for 1–2 minutes.
4. Gradually add milk, stirring until thick and smooth.
5. Stir in 3oz (75gm) cheese and continue stirring till cheese melts.
6. Layer the potatoes, bacon, eggs and sauce in a lightly buttered ovenware dish, ending with a layer of sauce.
7. Mix together remaining cheese and breadcrumbs and sprinkle on top.
8. Bake in centre of oven for about 30 minutes until topping is golden brown and crisp.
9. Serve with a crisp green salad.

RATATOUILLE
Serves 4

3 tablespoons salad oil
8oz (200gm) onions, chopped
1 garlic clove, finely chopped
2lb (1 kilo) courgettes, cubed
1½lb (¾ kilo) aubergines, cubed
1lb (½ kilo) tomatoes, peeled and diced
salt and pepper
parsley
thyme
1 bayleaf
8oz (200gm) long-grain rice
1 pint (approximately ½ litre) water
1 teaspoon salt

1. Preheat oven to very moderate, 325 deg F or gas 3 (170 deg C).
2. Heat salad oil in a frying pan, add onion and garlic and fry gently.
3. Add courgettes, aubergines and tomatoes.
4. Season with salt and pepper then add sprinkling of parsley, thyme and the bayleaf.
5. Pour into a casserole and cook in centre of oven for 30 minutes.
6. Meanwhile, put rice, water and salt into a saucepan.
7. Bring to the boil and stir once.
8. Lower heat to simmer, then cover and cook for 15 minutes until rice is tender.
9. Serve rice with ratatouille.

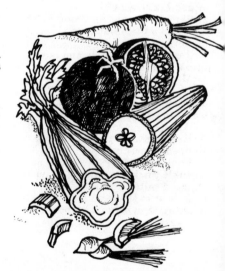

SUCCOTASH
(Illustrated on page 72)
Serves 6

1 medium can baked beans
1 medium can garden peas,
strained
1 medium can corn kernels
8oz (200gm) tomatoes, skinned
and quartered
few drops Worcestershire
sauce
1½ level teaspoons prepared
mustard
salt and pepper

1. Place all the ingredients in a
large saucepan.
2. Heat through gently for 5
minutes.
3. Serve at once with sausages or
hamburgers.

AURIOL
Serves 4

8oz (200gm) onions
1 large tomato
1 green pepper
1 can ham and chicken roll
1oz (25gm) dripping
1 packet frozen sweetcorn,
thawed
salt and pepper
2 dessertspoons mustard pickle

1. Peel the onions and slice
finely.
2. Slice the tomato and de-seed
and chop the green pepper.
3. Dice the ham and chicken roll.
4. Melt the dripping and fry the
onions until soft. Add the
tomato, green pepper and ham
and chicken.
5. Drain the sweetcorn, add to the
frying pan and heat thoroughly.
6. Season well and add the pickle.
7. Serve with boiled rice and a
green salad.

DEVILLED CORN
Serves 4

6 tablespoons milk
8oz (200gm) cheese, grated
½ beaten egg
4oz (100gm) cooked sweetcorn
½ teaspoon piquant table sauce
pinch of salt
2 slices bread
brown breadcrumbs
½oz (12gm) butter, melted
tomato slices to garnish

1. Preheat oven to hot, 425 deg F
or gas 7 (220 deg C).
2. Heat the milk and cheese
together. When smooth, remove
the pan from the heat.
3. Pour the egg into the mixture.
4. Add the corn, sauce and salt.
5. Cut the bread into small cubes
and add it to the corn.
6. Turn the mixture into greased
scallop shells.
7. Top with breadcrumbs and
butter and bake for about 20
minutes, until golden brown.
8. Serve hot, garnished with
tomato.

SWEETCORN PUFF
Serves 4

1½oz (37gm) butter
1½oz (37gm) flour
½ pint (250ml) milk
salt and pepper
4oz (100gm) fresh sweetcorn
1 teaspoon onion juice
1 level teaspoon chopped
parsley
3 egg yolks
4 egg whites

1. Preheat oven to moderately
hot, 400 deg F or gas 6 (200 deg C).
2. Melt the butter in a pan.
3. Add flour and cook for a
moment then remove from heat.
4. Blend in the milk and cook,
stirring well, for a few minutes.
5. Season. Add corn, onion juice
and parsley.
6. Cook for a few minutes,
stirring well.
7. Add egg yolks one at a time.
Whisk whites and fold into the
mixture. Turn into a greased
ovenproof dish.
8. Bake on second shelf from the
top of oven for 20 minutes. Serve
at once.

CANADIAN BAKED SWEETCORN
Serves 4

9 tablespoons tomato ketchup
½ level teaspoon dry mustard
pinch of salt
½oz (12gm) brown sugar
1 onion, chopped
1 can sweetcorn
4 streaky bacon rashers, diced

1. Preheat oven to moderate, 350
deg F or gas 4 (180 deg C).
2. Mix the tomato ketchup,
mustard, salt and brown sugar
together.
3. Stir in the onion and
sweetcorn and pour into a greased
ovenware dish.
4. Top with bacon and bake for 40
minutes or until the bacon is
cooked.

TOMATOES STUFFED WITH MACKEREL
Serves 4

1 can mackerel fillets
2 hard-boiled eggs
1 tablespoon bottled tomato
sauce
salt and pepper
8 medium tomatoes
lettuce leaves

1. Mash mackerel in a bowl using
a fork.
2. Slice hard-boiled eggs. Reserve
four slices for garnish and
chop remainder.
3. Add to fish, with sauce and mix
well. Season to taste.
4. Cut a thin slice from top of
each tomato and discard pips and
core. Fill tomatoes with mackerel
mixture.
5. Garnish top of each tomato
with a slice of egg.
6. Serve on a bed of lettuce.

Basic recipes

FRENCH DRESSING

4 tablespoons olive oil
½ level teaspoon salt
¼ level teaspoon caster sugar
¼ level teaspoon freshly
ground pepper
2 tablespoons white wine
vinegar

1. Put oil into a basin and add
salt, sugar and pepper.
2. Whisk in the vinegar drop by
drop and continue beating until
mixture thickens slightly.

Variations
Add a few chopped fresh herbs, a
little crushed garlic or a dash of
mustard etc.

ASPIC JELLY
Makes ½ pint or 250ml

½oz (12gm) gelatine
½ pint (250ml) boiling water
¼oz (6gm) caster sugar
¼ level teaspoon salt
2 tablespoons tarragon vinegar
2 tablespoons lemon juice

1. Dissolve gelatine in boiling
water. Add all other ingredients.
2. Leave to cool and thicken.
3. Use as required either before
or after it has set as the recipe
demands.

Note
Alternatively, thicken a can of
consommé with approximately 2
teaspoons gelatine. Or dilute clear
meat extract or a bouillon cube
with ½ pint (250ml) water and add
approximately 2 teaspoons
gelatine.

WHITE SAUCE
Makes ½ pint or 250ml

½oz (12gm) butter or margarine
½oz (12gm) flour
½ pint (250ml) cold milk (or
milk and stock or water mixed)
salt and pepper

1. Melt the butter or margarine
in a pan over a gentle heat.
2. Stir in flour and cook without
browning for 2 minutes, stirring
all the time.
3. Remove pan from heat and
gradually beat in the liquid.
Alternatively, add all the liquid
and whisk thoroughly.
4. Return to heat and bring to
boil, stirring well. Simmer gently
for 2–3 minutes and add
seasoning. If sauce is to be kept,
cover it with greaseproof paper or
foil to prevent a skin forming.

THICK WHITE SAUCE
Makes ½ pint or 250ml

Make exactly as for white sauce,
above, but double the quantities
of butter or margarine and flour
used.

CHEESE SAUCE
Makes ½ pint or 250ml

Make up ½ pint (250ml) white
sauce (see this page). After sauce
has come to the boil and
thickened, add 2–4oz (50–100gm)
grated cheese and ½ level
teaspoon mustard. Stir sauce over
low heat until cheese melts.

SHORTCRUST PASTRY
Makes 8oz or 200gm pastry

8oz (200gm) plain flour
1 level teaspoon salt
2oz (50gm) lard
2oz (50gm) butter or margarine
cold water to mix

1. Sift flour and salt into a bowl.
2. Cut fats into flour with a knife.
3. Rub fats into flour with
fingertips until mixture resembles
fine breadcrumbs.
4. Add water little by little,
stirring with a knife until mixture
forms large lumps.
5. Bring mixture together with
fingertips and knead lightly into a
ball.
6. Roll out briskly on a floured
board. Avoid stretching the
pastry.

Note
Baking temperature: moderately
hot, 400 deg F or gas 6 (200 deg C).

RICH SHORTCRUST PASTRY

Make as for shortcrust pastry,
above, but sift the flour with ½oz
(12gm) icing sugar and mix in 1
egg before adding the water.

Note
Baking temperature: moderate to
moderately hot, 375 deg F or gas 5
(190 deg C).

CHEESE PASTRY
Makes 8oz or 200gm pastry

Use for savoury pies, canapé bases, cheese straws and savoury flans.

8oz (200gm) self-raising flour
1 level teaspoon salt
pinch of cayenne pepper
2oz (50gm) lard
2oz (50gm) butter or margarine
5oz (125gm) cheese, grated
1–2 egg yolks
cold water to mix

1. Sift flour, salt and pepper into a bowl.
2. Cut fats into flour with a knife.
3. Rub fats into flour with fingertips until mixture resembles fine breadcrumbs. Add cheese.
4. Mix in egg, then add water little by little, stirring with a knife until mixture forms large lumps.
5. Bring mixture together with fingertips and knead lightly into a ball.
6. Roll out briskly on a floured board. Avoid stretching the pastry.

Note
Baking temperature: moderate, 350 deg F or gas 4 (180 deg C).

SUET CRUST PASTRY
Makes 8oz or 200gm pastry

Use for steak and kidney puddings, sweet puddings and roly polies.

8oz (200gm) self-raising flour or 8oz (200gm) plain flour plus 2 teaspoons baking powder
1 level teaspoon salt
4oz (100gm) beef or mutton suet, shredded or grated
¼ pint (125ml) cold water

1. Sift self-raising flour (or plain flour and baking powder) into a bowl with salt.
2. Add suet then mix in water with a knife until lumps begin to form.
3. Gather mixture lightly together and knead until smooth.
4. Turn out on a floured board and shape into a ball. Leave to stand 10 minutes before using.

Note
Baking temperature: moderately hot, 400 deg F or gas 6 (200 deg C). Alternatively, steam.

FLAKY PASTRY
Makes 8oz or 200gm pastry

Use for pies, vanilla slices, sausage rolls.

8oz (200gm) plain flour
1 level teaspoon salt
3oz (75gm) lard
3oz (75gm) butter or margarine
1 teaspoon lemon juice
water to mix

1. Sift flour and salt into a bowl. Blend the fats on a plate and mark into four portions.
2. Rub one portion into the flour until it resembles fine breadcrumbs.
3. Mix to a smooth dough with lemon juice and water.
4. Knead dough lightly and roll it out on a floured surface into an oblong.
5. Dot two-thirds of the pastry with second portion of fat.
6. Fold the bottom third up and the top third over into an envelope shape.
7. Allow pastry to relax for 10 minutes in a cold place. This is especially important in warm weather.
8. Repeat the whole process until all the fat is used up.
9. Fold pastry in two, roll out to ¼–½ inch thick and use as required.

Note
Baking temperature: hot, 425 deg F or gas 7 (220 deg C).

PUFF PASTRY
Makes 8oz or 200gm pastry

Use for vol au vents, bouchée cases, patties, mille feuilles, palmiers. It is essential to keep everything including hands very cold for this pastry.

8oz (200gm) plain flour
½ level teaspoon salt
8oz (200gm) unsalted butter in a block or 4oz (100gm) cooking fat and 4oz (100gm) margarine mashed and formed into a block
2 teaspoons lemon juice
6–8 tablespoons very cold water

1. Sift flour and salt into a bowl.
2. Chill the fat if soft. Rub ½oz (12gm) fat into flour.
3. Mix to a dough with lemon juice and water.
4. Roll out dough to twice the length of the block of fat. Place fat on dough and fold dough down over it, sealing edges well with a rolling pin.
5. Give pastry one half turn and roll gently out into a long strip.
6. Fold dough in three, envelope style, and leave, covered, in a cold place for 30 minutes.
7. Repeat turning, rolling and folding six times.
8. Leave pastry to relax for 30 minutes between rollings and before use.

Note
Baking temperature: hot, 450 deg F or gas 8 (230 deg C).

PANCAKE BATTER
Makes ½ pint or 250ml

4oz (100gm) plain flour
pinch of salt
1 egg
½ pint (250ml) cold milk
1 tablespoon oil

1. Sift flour and salt into a bowl.
2. Make a well in the centre and break egg into it.
3. Gradually beat in half the milk and continue beating until batter is smooth.
4. Fold in rest of milk with oil.

Index